THE

COMMON SENSE

OF INSANITY

A PATH TO CLARITY, SUCCESS AND HAPPINESS

AMEEN F ALMADEN

Printed in the United States of America

First Printing, 2020

ISBN 978-1-7359553-0-8

Dedication

This book is dedicated to all those who inspired me to start, persevere, and finish writing this book. Its dedicated to the music that inspired me and to the many cups of coffee and to the baristas who made them. Its dedicated to all the issues, problems, and experiences good and not that I went through. Its dedicated to you my dear, for picking up my book and browsing it thinking you might find something that will entertain you or benefit you in your life.

Table of Contents:

INTRODUCTION

Before you start reading the chapters of this book, let us agree that life is not a problem to be solved, but rather it's a rollercoaster ride and a journey that is meant to be lived and experienced, so be ready and buckle up.

You will find in this book some life navigation tips and guidelines. The chapters you are about to read will illustrate some methods and techniques that will help you in bringing about your own luck. It will provide some uniquely new but twisted points of view about life and death, experiencing and living life, happiness and depression, and love, and forgiveness. Reading the book will hopefully drive you into reaching the elusive happiness that you are constantly searching for.

This book is written in a way in which you can decide to pick it up every now and then to remind yourself of some valuable life lessons, guidelines, and tips to use and go by in life. There are a lot of aspects and experiences in this book that will hopefully help you in going through life with all its ups and downs the same way it has helped me. You can choose to read the book chapters chronologically, or you can pick and choose the chapter that interests and appeal to you without worrying about the order of the chapter. Using one of these different methods to read it will provide you with a different experience and with some valuable lessons combined with some needed new life skills. Keep in mind that the chapters in this book are meant to help not in finding one's self but rather is meant to help in molding, forming, and creating one's self. Don't expect answers to all the problems in the world because this book will likely leave you with more questions about yourself and about life than answers.

This book will discuss a range of topics, including happiness and depression, philosophy, and religions, life and death, and everything in between. Each chapter might give you an answer to a question that you might have, but it will definitely leave you with something to think about.

If you ever made some bad choices and ended up blaming or not forgiving yourself for those bad choices, then you will find something valuable in this book. If you ever achieved some or all of your goals in life and you are still struggling to be happy and to find or build a happy life, then you will find some excellent resources in this book that will guide you toward achieving just that. If you ever found it challenging to discover and form a purpose in your life or you found it hard to see the beauty and the perfection in this life, then you will find something in this book that will illustrate to you some methods and techniques which will ease you in doing just that. If you struggled trying to find success in your life and consequently depression found its way into your sphere, then keep on reading to pick up some techniques and approaches that hopefully will propel you into success and will rid you off that depressed state.

The goal of reading this book is to be able to face all of your obstacles and problems with force and an open mind. To be ready to embrace the process of building out your personality and future while at the same time, making sure you can find and form your purpose in this life. For without a purpose in life, you will never achieve the maximum happiness you can achieve in this world and this journey. Faith, hope, peace, forgiveness, leadership, life, and death are all elements, skills, and talents that you will pick up, gain, and learn in your life's journey that will assist you in navigating through life struggles and challenges. Just make sure to be resilient and open-minded, and embrace change as much as you fight it because difficult roads often lead to beautiful destinations. When your life gets tough, and things start going sideways, remember that sometimes you have to go up really high not from using drugs but from looking at your life with a bird's eye view literally by flying or imaginatively by closing your eyes and picturing that view to understand how small you alongside all of yours challenges and difficulties really are. Things will get better eventually, and life will move on with you stressing about it or not. However, no matter the experience you go through in life, one of the most important things that you must keep on doing is the act of asking questions and contemplating your life in order for you to become a better you.

PART ONE

Becoming a better you

CHAPTER ONE

Learning how, who, and when to follow

> **""**
>
> Life will change everyone, but it will take a special one to change life.

Every human being was born to lead. Yes, you are born to lead, and not necessarily to lead others but to lead and to take control of yourself and your own life. Taking a leadership role in your own life is so vital for you to grow and mature in life. Doing so allows you to bring out your best, and it enables you to attract joy and happiness. It also teaches you how to become a more responsible person and how to be better at handling different situations, good and bad. By taking a leadership role in your own life, you become better at decision-making, and even more so at accepting and taking ownership of the consequences of those decisions. Do yourself a service and decide to take a leadership role in your own life. Start setting your personal goals, making your own decisions, and mistakes along the way, pushing through your failures, learning from your mistakes, and improving your leadership skills as well as your own life.

Good leaders show their leadership by following.

When it comes to being a leader and taking a leadership role, be it in other's or your own life, you never just stumble upon the ability of being a leader. Leadership, on its own, is a talent. Some people are born with it, while others need to learn and study at it to be good and master it. You can quickly figure out if you are a natural-born leader or not by looking into and examining some characteristics that exist in every natural-born leader. Characteristics such as a passion for leadership, an ability to energize and galvanize teams and followers, and an ability to stay even-keeled and handle situations, good and bad, positively. Some are born with desires and passion for leading, while others are promoted and or involuntary pushed into becoming leaders. There are many examples where people are put into leadership roles while lacking the skills that go with it. You can see it at work where a person will get promoted into a manager and leadership role just because of the number of years they spent at the company and not because of their leadership skills. You can see it happen when people are born into a leadership role, such as when a person inherits a company and must lead that company moving forward. Additionally, you can also see people involuntarily pushed into a leadership role, such as leading a team just based on their on-field skills and talent and not for their leadership skills.

There are stark differences between a natural-born leader and those trained to be leaders, and those differences are not hard to spot. Natural leaders are born with a passion for leading and usually will take pride in voicing their opinions and articulating their points of view. They will never shy away from dominating and showing their alpha mentality. They tend to lead not only by example and by doing the work themselves but also by preaching, pushing forward, and making sure to bring their team or followers along the way. Furthermore, they can keep themselves in check and can easily control their emotions and understand what buttons to push and when to push them, to get their team or their followers motivated and inspired. The combination of these characteristics is known as having a charismatic personality, which is again not easy to come by. Even if you are considered a good leader, you can still lack the charismatic aspect of it.

All fields and disciplines have leaders and followers. This world has so many different types of leaders in so many fields and disciplines. They can range from a country's president, a religious leader, an airplane pilot, to a basketball captain. No matter the field or the discipline, there are always guidelines, principles, and rules that govern each field or discipline. In most cases, good leaders will make sure to follow these rules and laws. In other cases, a team member can suggest a better way to accomplish the same principle, and a good leader will show his or her leadership by their willingness to amend those guidelines and by following the team member's suggestion. Being a good leader does not mean giving out the first and only decision. Instead, it means showing confidence and inspiring others to provide input and solutions while communicating clearly and honestly to eventually, and as a good leader, be able to make a firm decision and be accountable for it.

You should work on training and improving the leader within yourself. The worst thing a person can do to himself or herself is to be a blind follower. Being a blind follower is like closing your eyes and jumping off a cliff without knowing what's under that cliff and whether there is a chance for survival or not. Surviving the jump here can be physical, in some cases, like using drugs because your acquaintance asked you to join. In other cases, mental and spiritual, like blindly believing in ideologies or practicing a religion and following a religious leader just because your parents do. Again, you never work on the leader within yourself and you become a blind follower then you allow yourself to be like a ghost ship wandering around in an open ocean. You are wandering without any direction, not knowing where you are going, or if you are even going to survive the journey. Being a blind follower means that you are binding yourself to eventually sinking to the bottom of the deep, deep ocean like all the other ghost ships and blind followers that continue to fill up the bottom of the oceans.

Knowledge is non-transferable by association only, beliefs are. Beliefs are way easier to transfer than knowledge. In life, you can be brought up in a certain area or within a certain tradition or community. From there, you start believing and picking up those community beliefs and traditions. On the contrary, you can live with or surround yourself with scientists, but you will not and should not expect to pick up their knowledge without actually making an effort to learn and obtain that knowledge. If knowledge were transferable by association only, the world would be more advanced, and humans would have been able to achieve and reach an ideal world if there is a chance that it even exists.

If a million people say one thing, that does not make it correct or accurate. You have a brain and mind to learn, and intuition to differentiate right from wrong. You, as a human being, are blessed since birth with mind, soul, and intuition. As long as your soul and identity are still not corrupted by any outside factors such as hate, greed, and other social factors, then you can easily differentiate between right and wrong. Being a blind follower means you decided to ignore all the brainpower you have, and you succumbed to all the socially available and accessible ideologies and beliefs. These socially accessible ideologies depend on where you come from and what times you have lived through. Some of these ideologies and beliefs might be accurate, but a lot are either bogus or just debatable. Therefore, you will need to use your mind and intuition to find the truth for yourself, and only by doing so will you do yourself the ultimate justice.

If someone sounds articulate and knowledgeable about a certain subject, that does not mean that they are smart and that what they are saying is accurate. You cannot judge a person's intelligence by the amount of education they have or the number of degrees and certificates they own. Being educated or having a higher degree does not mean a person is smarter than any other person. It just means that they might have more knowledge about a certain subject than other people. In some cases, having more knowledge is not necessarily an advantage because having that knowledge without the proper experience of using that knowledge is the same as having none at all. You can spend a few years reading and learning about how to build a house. Still, without a real experience going through the process and the ups and downs, and the success and failures of building a house, you cannot really utilize and benefit from all the knowledge you had accumulated through years of studying.

On the other hand, possessing knowledge alongside some experience can also hinder your growth and development. Each experience you go through provides you with different types of results and emotions. These results and emotions will contribute to your decision-making moving forward. As a human being, you try to avoid the sensation of pain, be it physical or psychological. So, when you go through experiences that give you a feeling of disdain or evoke painful memories, you try to choose different paths moving forward for you to avoid any future pain and disdain. By avoiding certain paths based on prior painful or bad experiences, you allow your experiences to control and interfere with your decision-making moving forward. You allow it to prevent you from using certain routes and from taking risks that might benefit you or your business better. Allowing your disdain of painful experiences to affect your decision-making will prevent you from taking risks in life that might end up making a positive change in yours as well as others' lives. Therefore, to be a good leader in life, you will need to balance your education and experience because having one without the other is like owning a bicycle without knowing how to ride it. For that bicycle to run, you will need to push off one foot (your education) and then the other foot (your experience), and so forth in a balanced pace.

You can be a natural-born leader with a passion for leadership and the required energy to galvanize and energize your team and followers. You can easily maintain an even-keeled relationship with success and failures, and you can handle each member, follower, or situation fairly and evenly. Certainly, being born with those characteristics will contribute significantly in molding you into a great leader. However, being born a leader is not a requirement for you to be a good leader. If you are not a natural-born leader, you can still learn and train yourself to become a good leader. You do that by sharpening your human interaction skills and honing your ability to assess and study each situation while polishing your decision-making skills at the same time.

Yet, with all that and whether you are a natural-born leader or not, for you to master the art of being a good leader, you will need to pedal with your knowledge's feet ahead of your beliefs. Your knowledge, above everything else, except imagination, should drive your leadership. By no means, you should stop believing. Rather, you should lean toward using your knowledge before beliefs. On your way toward knowledge, you will pick up or drop so many different beliefs to integrate into or remove from your life and your decision-making. Your beliefs are just one element alongside learning and intuition that will help in building out your knowledge. So, keep on learning, believing, and gaining more knowledge and experiences to avoid becoming a blind follower and to show your leadership by being decent, inspiring, and accountable.

Tips on taking leadership of your own life and becoming a better leader in general:

- Train yourself to become a more compassionate and empathic leader to understand the people you are leading and to identify what makes them motivated and inspired.

- Simulate and put yourself through a variety of situations to better yourself and improve your decision-making abilities.

- Work on improving and honing your ability to control your emotions so that you can be better equipped at handling and dealing with high-pressure situations when that time comes.

- Learn to balance your knowledge, experience, and faith, doing so will propel you into becoming a better decision-maker and, consequently, a better leader.

- Learn to lead by following, amending the guidelines, and allowing team members to take the lead not out of necessity but rather for the betterment of the team and the situation at hand.

CHAPTER TWO

Discovering your talent and learning to wield it

"

> You can be considered talented without accomplishing anything, but you cannot be called genius without revolutionizing and achieving so many accomplishments in a certain field or a particular profession.

Why are you doing that? Why do you make sure to set aside time to read, to check your email, to check your social media accounts, to eat, to shower, to sleep but never to think and reflect?

You go through life, and you make sure to set aside a time for all and every action in your life, and yet you forget or intentionally ignore setting aside a time to think and reflect about yourself and your own life. You are not alone in this, and most people go through life and their daily and weekly routines without setting aside a time to think and reflect on their lives. You go through life trying to set aside money to invest in buying real estate or stocks. You are probably setting aside time to complete a certain action, such as watching, reading, studying, training, sleeping, and other similar activities. You do all those actions thinking that by doing them, you are preparing for your future and working on improving yourself and your life. Yet, in reality, you are preparing for your death, because what you need to realize is that death does not only happen when your heart stops beating inside your chest. It can happen when you are hopeless with a dark future, and when you are just waiting for nothing to happen and enduring extreme boredom. If you are not regularly setting aside money or time to invest or think about yourself, your purpose and your goals, then you are just leading yourself to a life lacking any meaning or purpose full of disappointment, and hopelessness.

Commit yourself to routinely setting aside some money to invest in yourself, be it your education, travel, or putting yourself through new experiences. Additionally, alongside investing money into improving yourself, make sure to set aside a time to think about yourself and to reflect on your life, your purpose, and how to work toward achieving and improving them. The more money and time you spend on yourself, the more gains and rewards you will receive. Once you can think clearly and you can connect to your internal self, you will be able to find your purpose, talent, and passion in life. By finding the talent and realizing the thing or things that give you hope and life, and as long as you invest in them, you will consequently receive all the gains from those investments. You will be able to enjoy life, and you will be able to fill it with joy, purpose, and happiness, all of which would not be possible without you taking the time and thinking and reflecting. So many aspects of your life rely on you finding the thing which you are talented in or in other words, the thing that you are born to do. You might discover that you are already talented, a genius, or you can dedicate yourself to becoming talented at something. Hence, you will need to be able to know and understand the differences between being talented, a genius, or both.

Being talented means having or gaining an outstanding set of skills, techniques, and abilities, doing and excelling at a certain thing, whereas, being a genius means having an exceptional intellectual or creative power improving and enhancing a certain subject. There are a lot of differences between a talented person and a genius person. A lot of people, including you, are already talented in something, be it playing sports, video games, writing, reading, cooking, or any other talent. If you can't come up with a talent for yourself, I am here to tell you that you can always be talented at something, and all you need is a solid commitment and a proper dedication. You will eventually be talented at that which you seek to be talented in. However, being talented is one thing, and being a genius is a completely different thing. Talent is teachable, whereas genius is natural and can't be taught. You can find any skill or talent you want to learn. With the proper resources and dedication, I can guarantee that you will eventually achieve a skill level to that which is associated with talented people, if not more. Now, whether you have the dedication to achieve a skill level to that of talented people, is not guaranteed, because dedication on its own is a skill that's not easy to come by.

There are people born with talent; then, there are those who become talented through hard work and dedication to their craft. Those with natural-born talent win the debate of who is better when comparing them with those people who gained their talent through hard work and dedication, especially if the natural-born talent worked as hard as the other group did. In life, you can be talented without being a genius, but you cannot be a genius without being talented. A person can be described as talented without accomplishing any work or achievements. Whereas for a person to be called a genius, he or she is required to have a collection of work or achievements that he or she has accomplished, which in turn can help in inserting their names in the genius discussion. For genius people to have these types of accomplishments, he or she needs some type of talent to co-exist and enhance their genius.

Talent is measurable and comparable, whereas genius is not measurable nor comparable. You can examine and compare any two humans with the same talent, and based on certain classification such as performance, originality, or time; you can deduce who has more talent between the two at the time of the comparison. On the other hand, genius is not comparable. If you take two people who are considered geniuses in a certain field, you will not be able to deduce who is more genius than the other because each of these geniuses is unique in their own way. Both have come up with something unique and outstanding to lift and elevate the field they are in. One big difference between talent and genius is that talent is undeniable. If a person is talented in a field, no one can deny or dismiss their talent, whereas genius is perspective and based on interpretation. You can call a person genius because what you have seen or read about them, and because of what your intuition deduced about them. At the same time, others can call them lunatic because of what they have seen from them, or according to what their intuition deduced about them.

Additionally, talent can diminish with time if not practiced, sharpened, and honed. On the other hand, genius does not require constant practicing and honing and will stay ready and accessible for whenever the person decides to tap into it. Finally, a talented person will be able to use his or her skills and techniques to accomplish a certain outcome or achieve a positive result in doing or performing a task. That same talented person has accomplished the same task many times before. Still, he or she will try to perform and accomplish a better result whenever they use their skills to accomplish the same task again. Whereas, a genius person will accomplish and come up with a result no one else except he or she could ever imagine, let alone achieve.

In this world, there are more talented people than there are talented geniuses. For a person to be a talented genius, he or she needs to have an outstanding set of skills that will allow him or her to outperform and outdo the competition. They will also need to have a natural ability to improvise, invent, and predict the outcome. So, now that you can differentiate between being talented or a genius, you can find that at which you are talented in or wish to be talented in. With hard work and dedication, you will be able to reach your goals and exceed them eventually. With proper dedication and proper motivation, you, as well as anyone else, can achieve being talented at something if you or they put their mind and heart into it. Lastly, remember that being talented or genius at one thing does not mean that your talent or genius will apply to all aspects of your life. Meaning, you can be a talented person in a sport or a genius individual in composing art, but you can still be lacking sufficient skills in most other areas of life. So, never settle for less, and aspire for your talent to influence all other aspects of your life, and always aim for the best when it comes to producing results.

Some tips and methods to help you with honing your talent:

- Find proper motivation to push you toward that which you wish to be good at.

- Some of the most important commodities in this world are time and money. The more you invest them on yourself, the more gains and rewards you will receive, and the better and stronger your talent and passion will shine through you.

- Read success stories to learn and pick up some helpful and useful lessons and research failure stories to learn from mistakes and how to avoid or mitigate them.

- Don't shy away from asking those people who have a similar talent for advice and pointers.

- Celebrate all the milestones you achieve, the small ones before the big ones.

CHAPTER THREE

Realizing and achieving greatness

> "
>
> Greatness has to come from within and with the goal of
> inspiring others.

A lot of people go through life thinking and dreaming of the great things they will do and accomplish in their lives. However, in reality, only a few will be able to achieve some or all of their hopes and dreams. Those who can accomplish all the great things they thought and dreamed of doing, do so not because they were lucky in their lives, but because they fought and persisted using everything within them and everything they had to create their own luck and to succeed. At the core of achieving greatness and the main pillar that will aid you in fulfilling all the great things you dream of is belief. Everything else will follow your belief, and without it, you or your accomplishments will never reach the greatness you seek and search for. Therefore, for you and your actions to achieve the greatness you dream of, you must believe in yourself and in your ability to reach greatness. However, most importantly, you must believe in the thing you do or are about to do.

Greatness, what it is and where you get it from, is not a known constant. It's a variable, and therefore, there is no unified standard definition for greatness or for people and actions who are great, and there should not be one. Greatness is not like finding a unicorn but rather it's a blue moon shining its light every once in a while. Greatness can be hard to come by or reach, but it's not limited to a select few, and everyone has the chance to achieve it. Greatness is not purchasable, no matter how much money or influence you have. However, it's attainable by all people, and it's just a matter of finding out that passion or gift that keeps you fired up and ready to challenge all the obstacles to make your dreams become a reality. Greatness, whether in people or the actions they do or accomplish, has no standard definition, but it has some common characteristics. There are a lot of characteristics that are associated with great people and great actions, and the following examples are essential for achieving greatness: obsession, resiliency, sacrifice, inspiration, and imagination.

Obsession

For you and for your accomplishments to reach greatness, a certain level of obsession is required. You need to be obsessed with what you do, go to sleep thinking about it and wake up thinking about it. You will realize when you have reached that proper level of obsession when others start thinking that you are nearing insanity, but only you know that you are still sane but with a proper level of obsession. You become so involved in the thing you are trying to accomplish to the point where you eventually start ignoring and or forgetting to eat. You and others are born with a gift, and it's a matter of realizing it, working with it, and on it, to reach its potential and beyond. For you and for your talent or skill to achieve greatness, you need to love what you do and pour your heart and soul into what you do, be it sports, singing, writing, science, or cooking. By doing this, you unlock one of the secrets for your work and your greatness to reach, touch, and affect people.

You need to understand that to achieve greatness; you will need to believe in what you do and not what you are going to get from doing it. Believe and love what you do regardless of whether you are going to get a financial return from it or not. Whatever it is that you are doing, just make sure to do it with passion and pour all your feelings and emotions into it, and only then can you start knocking on the door of greatness. A lot of great people, artists, and leaders throughout history faced a lot of challenges at the beginning of their journeys to greatness. They failed and failed again and again, but they believed in themselves and the things, art, messages they produced, accomplished, and fought for. They did so without setting personal gain as a goal of theirs. They did so without knowing that their art or messages would be greatly valued monetarily or symbolically to this day. They only did so because they knew that what they did was great and fulfilling to them and because they believed and loved what they did. Hence, their work is still being collected, celebrated, and studied and will be for many years to come.

Resiliency

"I never lose; either I win, or I learn a new lesson." Nelson Mandela

To achieve greatness, you must endure the toughness and the cruelty of the path to greatness. The path to greatness is full of obstacles and challenges that you will have to go through and sometimes repeatedly to overcome the current obstacle and move on to the next challenge. Those challenges, obstacles, failures, and successes are all part of the process of achieving your greatness. To achieve greatness, you must look for and be excited about your failures as much as you get excited about your successes. Just make sure to learn from any failure you go through and celebrate any success you come by. Additionally, there are two types of failures that you need to be able to distinguish between: the bad useless failure and the good useful failure. The bad failure can happen in so many different ways and under different circumstances. An example is when you fail and never learn from your failures, and when you doubt yourself by discouraging yourself from facing any challenges. Bad failures happen when you start saying things like, "I can do it if I wanted to do it," or "I am just lazy to do it," or when you start saying, "it cannot be done" and admit defeat without even trying. On the other hand, the good failure is the one that you should be excited about, the actionable failure. The actionable failure is good because you are at least trying to challenge yourself to do something, even if you still fail. The former is bad because you don't gain anything from it other than wasting your potential. Whereas, the latter failure is good for you because any failed action or experiment is just the natural path to achieving success and greatness. Aspire to become so resilient and at peace with all the challenges and issues in your life. Once you reach that pinnacle, you will be able to feel numb toward all the challenges that life throws at you, and you will be unfazed toward any issue or problem that you might face. By becoming at peace with any challenge or issue in your life, you, in turn, become better at controlling the situation, fixing the issue, and going through the challenge without any trouble, like it's casual Friday. You develop an ability that allows you to normalize all the struggles in your life and all the other challenges, physical or not that accompanies those struggles. They become normalized to the point where you will need someone else to alert you of the great achievements you are accomplishing while dealing with all those challenges and issues like a champ and without any complaints. There are many examples where you can see normalization of struggles and challenges in your own daily life or in others. Examples of such normalization of physical challenges can appear while watching the great things all handicapped Olympians do in their sports competitions. They don't see the physical challenge of missing a limb, for instance, as a challenge or a struggle. Rather, you or anyone else looking in from the outside, not knowing what it means or how it feels to be handicapped, can tell that what they are doing and achieving is extremely remarkable. Thus, regardless of the issue or the challenge you are facing, just keep on pushing yourself and trying not only harder, but most importantly, smarter. Even if constant failure is bringing you pain, don't let the pain stop or deter you from reaching your goal. Understand that pain is just a temporary feeling. It might last for a week or a month, but eventually, you will either get used to it to the point where it does not affect you anymore, or it will subside, and the pain will turn into unprecedented joy. Therefore, make sure to keep reminding yourself that at the end of pain is success and heavenly gratification.

You go through life, hearing all kinds of discouraging and hurtful words from everyone around you, including yourself. The main purpose of these words in your life is to shatter your hopes and dreams. Hurtful words like, "you can't," "you won't," "not smart," "not intelligent," "have no talent," and "doubt." There will always be people around you, from friends, family, and "frenemies" whose sole purpose in being in your life is to plant doubt and hopelessness in you and within your desires. Every time you flap your wings against the wind and face a new challenge, they are there to make sure to throw stones at you. They are there to break your wings and to prevent you from achieving and fulfilling your potential.

There are also additional obstacles in your daily life that frustrate and discourage you from following your dreams and ambitions. Those obstacles can range from lack of financial resources, time, and opportunities, to the lack of physical, and emotional support. These obstacles are only examples of what you could be facing in your journey toward achieving greatness. Yet, you, alongside others, all have one common "frenemy" and one common obstacle. This common frenemy is always the first person to doubt and discourage you from achieving greatness. This frenemy is so talented and creative when it comes to planting hopelessness in you. The creativity level with this frenemy is so advanced, he/she can get an Oscar for it. This person who holds this much evil creativity and talent is none other than yourself. Yes, it's you, the person reading this book. You, as well as others, all have this evil creative person within you. Just ask yourself how many times you have doubted yourself and your abilities. How many times you have stopped yourself from doing or trying something because you thought you couldn't do it, or you told yourself you could have done it if you wanted to. All these thoughts are just the simplest examples of the creativity that your alter ego possesses. Your alter ego will win eighty percent of the time, and until you forcefully reverse that to the point where you are winning 80 percent of the time, you will not achieve your greater self and full potential. With all the obstacles and frenemies in your life, your alter ego is your main and fiercest obstacle. Don't let your alter ego stop you from what you want to do or where you want to be in life. Compete with yourself and make sure to win all the time, because whenever you win the competition with yourself, outside competition will never be able to harm or deter you.

Sacrifice

"Greatness is not an object you can just come by or pick up easily."

If you want to reach greatness, you should approach life, aspiring for all the good in the world. You will always have to work and sacrifice for that which you hope and desire in this life. Sometimes, rather than getting a reward for your sacrifices, you end up facing even more challenges. Yet, those challenges are part of your journey toward greatness, and no one said reaching the mountain top was easy. Therefore, for you to get closer to greatness, you need to sacrifice for it. Certainly, the type of sacrifice varies depending on you as a person, on your goals, and situation. More often, it would be time that you have to sacrifice. Other times, it can be health or relationships, and in extreme cases, it can be a combination of items and essentials. You or your actions will never achieve greatness without sacrifices because your greatness will need an adjective that is going to describe it, and your sacrifice is that adjective you will need. Thus, every great act and each great person in history is associated with a great sacrifice. There are many examples of great people or great acts through history, and we will go through some well-known but fairly recent examples of great people and great acts.

Nelson Mandela sacrificed over 20 years of his freedom, health, and time to constitute and kick-start democracy in South Africa. Mandela had many challenges and obstacles that could have forced him to change his views and beliefs during his prison time. Yet, with all the opportunities to quit and jump ship and switch his position to gain his freedom back, he still declined all of these opportunities and stuck with his beliefs, ideologies, and principles. His passion and belief in the democratic cause, accompanied by his many sacrifices, allowed him and his cause to prevail, and make him a household name, known for his great acts and great sacrifices.

Another example known for her sacrifice is Mother Teresa. She had to sacrifice her time, comfortable living, and health to do what she believed in and what she had passion and compassion for. Those two examples show that a person does not need extraterrestrial power or extraordinary physical power to achieve greatness. Both examples had a big heart and infinite passion for what they loved to do and what they believed in. Both characteristics are not easy to have or come by, but they do exist within all of us. So, make sure to utilize your big heart and find that infinite passion, which will lead you to achieve greatness.

Inspiration

When going about finding and achieving greatness, being inspired is a must, and striving to inspire yourself and others is a requirement. You achieve greatness when you or your actions get recognized and praised for their effects and influence on whatever field or subject you or your action is associated with. You reach greatness when you or your actions aid or inspire others to go through their life journey or to be great themselves. The effect and the inspiration you give to others is the best reward you can receive from all the hard work and the greatness you achieve. Therefore, make sure never to lose sight of the goal of inspiring others while working on achieving your greatness.

Additionally, make sure to find your muse, that person, or force that will stir your drive and creativity. Finding your muse is important because it will help you unlock the power of your imagination, and it will stir your resiliency and desire. Your muse could be a person, a story, or it could be nature, life, or even death. No matter the object, or the thing that inspires you to challenge yourself, you still need to find it and keep it within sight, physically or mentally. Having those muses within sight will make it easier for you to wake up every day motivated and driven to face any challenge or obstacle on your journey to greatness. Again, humans are creatures of habit, and these muses act as a constant reminder of that thing you are striving and pushing to achieve. Eventually, those muses become infused into your imagination, and consequently, help in planting the seed of faith, which is required to help kick-start your greatness. You need to have faith in yourself, alongside belief in what you do, as well as an infinite confidence that your big dreams and goals have greatness within them and that they will eventually materialize and lead you to greatness. Then and only then will others start believing in what you do, and they will be able to see greatness in you and your actions.

Imagination

"Imagination is more important than knowledge. For knowledge is limited, whereas imagination embraces the entire world, stimulating progress, giving birth to evolution" Albert Einstein.

Imagination is essential, and so is knowledge, and rather than figuring out which is more important, we can all agree that knowledge and imagination go hand-in-hand and drive and stimulate each other. The more knowledge you have, the more freedom and liberty your imagination will have.

The secret to achieving greatness is imagination. Imagination is the powerful entity that makes you visualize your life and future. Simply put, imagination is your own virtual reality, and you can create whatever story, life, and future you want because it's the only place where you have a decent amount of control over your life. Using your imagination, you can fly with or without wings, jump in a fire and come out unscathed, walk on water, have a full-on conversation with your pets, rule the world, or if you are married, maybe rule over your house for once. Imagination has no boundaries if you don't set or define boundaries for it.

Furthermore, to achieve greatness, you must see and envision not what you are now, but what you will become in the future, in ten years, or even in twenty years. Additionally, alongside using your imagination, make sure always to use your unfulfilled desires as fuel, because they are the driving force for your imagination and daydreaming. Your desire and passion for something will make your creativity and imagination go wild. You may have heard of Newton's third law of motion: "For every action, there is an equal and opposite reaction." This law applies to ignite your imagination and to fuel it with your desires. The more desire and passion you bring to your ultimate despair, the stronger and more creative your imagination becomes. Therefore, since your desires and passions are important in keeping your imagination and creativity flowing, you will need to make sure that your desires keep on burning, and your passion stays hot.

Different people respond and react to different things. Therefore, if knowing your goals and visualizing the outcome will keep your desires burning, then go ahead and use that as a motivation to keep them burning. Additionally, you can use self-reward, one of the simplest ways to keep your passion burning. The concept of self-reward or immediate gratification is not hard to understand, for the simple fact that human beings are creatures of habits. The same idea applies to animals as well. If you ever had a pet, you will understand that concept even more. For your pet to listen to you, obey your command, or do the trick you are trying to teach them; you will need to reward them whenever they obey or do that trick. This simple reward-based system applies to animals as well as to humans. In life, for a person to do a particular job, you pay them a salary, whereas, when it comes to keeping your desires burning and your passion hot, the only value accepted is pleasure and immediate gratification. Find that which brings joy and instant gratification to yourself and use it as a reward and an incentive to keep your passion and desires alive and burning.

Furthermore, remember that accomplishments and milestones differ in size and magnitude. They could be as small as finishing a chapter in a book you are writing or running two miles. On the other hand, they can be as big as finishing a book or quitting a bad habit. Regardless of the size and magnitude of the accomplishment, it's still important to celebrate the small accomplishments before the big ones, because doing so will keep you going and push you to accomplish and reach more. There are many ways to reward yourself for accomplishing anything in this life. You can do that by splurging on yourself and buying things if you have the means to do so, or if you love food, reward yourself with the best food after each accomplishment. You must celebrate and reward yourself after each accomplishment because gratification and happiness will keep your desires alive and wanting more, which, in turn, will help drive your imagination.

The unknown road to greatness

Unknowns and uncalculated events are an integral part of the road to greatness, and you must surpass them to reach the greatness you are looking for. You don't have to be perfect to achieve greatness. The more you accept your imperfections, the higher your chance of reaching greatness. Once you use your imperfections to your advantage, and once you learn to use them to push yourself toward your goals, you will ultimately be knocking on greatness' door.

Lastly, you need to understand that greatness in people or their actions are not comparable. You can always break down and compare the characteristics of great acts or great people. However, you will not be able to compare the greatness of actions or the greatness of people in their totality and decide and declare that one act or person is greater than another. Each one of them is great in their own way and their own time. You have to keep in mind that what's great for you is not as great for others, because at the end of the day, we all see or feel greatness differently, and that's why there is no universal definition for it.

A simple guide and plan for you to achieve greatness

- Discover your sanity level and then push yourself outside of your comfort zone to the end of your limits and make sure to come back sane, alive, and victorious.

- Push for success and be prepared for failure and setbacks. Understand that these failures and setbacks are the things that will propel you into greatness. If reaching the mountain top was easy, and without any obstacles, then it wouldn't be great. Therefore, think and dream big but start with small steps. Break your big dreams down into small manageable phases.

- To realize and recognize your path toward greatness, you will need to find your inspiration in life, be it in art, life, or people around you. You need to have your muse in your sight at all times and use them for inspiration to be able to inspire others with your greatness eventually.

- Make sure to set aside time to create your future using your imagination as a virtual reality engine. Once the vision of your future is clear, make sure to act upon it.

- Live the current day as if it was your last day, and remember that you are your own biggest enemy. The only way for you to lose is by not trying.

- Push yourself to be better. Get rid of your bad habits by thinking and running through your rock-bottom scenario and realize the seriousness of their consequences.

- Always celebrate your accomplishments, the small ones before the big ones.

- Assuming greatness is at 100%, you can assign 20% to each element: obsession and resiliency, sacrifice, inspiration, and imagination. Then decide which element you lack the most in and work on improving it until you reach at least 15% of the available 20%, and so on until the next factor.

CHAPTER FOUR

Saving yourself by forgiving it

"

Forgive the experience, but never forget the experience.

Are you a magician, a sorcerer, or a miracle-maker? Unless you are one of those and you can travel back to your past and change all that you deem to be a mistake or wrong made by you or others, then you should forgive yourself and others for all those wrongs and mistakes from your past. There is no sense in punishing your present and future time for your past mistakes since you are not gaining anything by doing so. So, make sure to just learn from those mistakes and wrongs, then forgive yourself and others for making them, grow from them, and then let go of them. By letting them vaporize from your heart and your world, you give yourself a bigger chance of being able to move on from them, and consequently, you allow yourself to become a better and stronger you.

Forgiveness is a sign of loving yourself. The more you forgive yourself and others, the more love you show to yourself. On the other hand, punishing yourself and others for past mistakes or bad choices and judgments made by you or by others toward you will only leave you with lasting damage that will ruin your judgment of the present and negatively affect your future outlook. Those mistakes can differ in size and magnitude. They can range from choosing the wrong career for yourself to placing your trust in the wrong people and getting betrayed and heartbroken as a result.

However, regardless of the size and magnitude of the mistake and in order for you to avoid lasting damage to your soul, heart, body, and overall health, you will be better off forgiving yourself and others for those past wrongs and mistakes. In most cases, it can be extremely difficult to forgive yourself or others for all the mistakes you did or the wrongs they did toward you. Yet, by committing yourself to doing just that, and by being generous with your forgiveness to yourself and others, you are ultimately the bigger beneficiary and winner. By forgiving yourself alongside others who wronged you, you are deciding to replace all the angst and anger within you with calmness of the heart and mind. You are choosing to have a better understanding of yourself and others, and consequently, receiving a wholesome realization of some of life's toughest and most valuable lessons along the way. Showing forgiveness to yourself and to those who wronged you and removing all the angst and anger from your heart, mind, and life will have a great benefit on your overall health. It will open your heart and attract more peacefulness and love to fill that empty spot that just opened. The more forgiveness you show to yourself and others, the more love you have for yourself. You are choosing to let bygones be bygones and choosing to continue living your life to the fullest without any dark clouds, and without anything anchoring you down and preventing you from moving ahead with your life.

Ships never sink because of all the water surrounding them. They sink because of that water leaking into them. Therefore, don't allow stress, grudges, and worries be the water leaking into your ship, or in this case, your heart. You will always be surrounded with worries, stress, and grudges as you go through life with its ups and downs. You will encounter many different people and personalities, and yet, you should never allow these matters and issues to have a damaging effect on you, your life, or your happiness. Learn to deal with life's different stages and issues, and aspire to be skilled in the art of letting go and forgiving. One important aspect which will help you in forgiving yourself and others for all the past mistakes, or the wrong turns you took in life, is your ability to realize and understand that nobody in this life is perfect. At some point in life, everyone, including you, will eventually make a mistake.

Furthermore, recognize that in your journey of life, you might learn some life lessons without making any mistakes. Still, you will understand and learn better by making them, going through them, and recognizing their effect on you and others. Understand that not only time will change and people will grow and mature, but you will also change, grow, and mature. You will keep on growing and maturing, especially if you allow yourself to go through all the different experiences needed for your maturation while at the same time, trying to learn all that they have to offer, the good and the bad. Hence, you should allow yourself to make some mistakes in life because it's an integral part of everyone's maturation process. However, to prevent your ship from sinking, it will be vital for you to learn from those mistakes and then decide to forgive yourself and others for those past mistakes, even if those actions seem unforgivable at the time. Forgiving yourself and others will kick-start your happiness and will allow it to flourish and radiate from within you and throughout your life.

In life, you need to go through a range of good and bad emotions, experiences, and issues for you to grow and get stronger mentally, emotionally, and physically. However, for you to come out stronger from these experiences, you will need to pick up and learn some important mental and physical skills and abilities. Picking up those needed skills will help you in navigating your life without sinking, and with yourself intact and stronger than ever. One of the most important skills that you need to learn is the ability to forgive yourself and let go of past mistakes. You start with learning how to forgive yourself, and once you do that, it will be easier for you to forgive others' mistakes toward you. Keep in mind that forgiving and forgetting are two different things, and you can do one without doing the other. You can and should forgive, but you should never forget. You should learn to forgive yourself for the mistakes and the bad experiences and choices you made in your life. By letting go of things anchoring you down, you allow yourself to move on in life and give yourself the ability to look for a better tomorrow. On the other hand, you should not forget those mistakes and bad experiences and choices. Remembering those mistakes, choices, and experiences, and grasping every lesson and moral they provide, is important for you to become more prepared for whatever life throws at you and to become a better you.

Your life is like the open sea, and you are a traveling ship in that moody sea with all of its silence- and sunny-filled days or raging dark nights. Your worries, stress, and grudges are the anchor or the rudder that controls whether your ship sails through that sea or not. A ship without an anchor will not be complete as it will never be able to dock in the harbor because the sea winds and waves will move it away. Your worries, stress, and grudges are your anchor or rudder, and you will need to experience them and learn from them to progress in your life.

You need to master when to lower your anchor, when to lift it up, and when to cut it off. You lower your anchor in an issue to find and come up with a solution. You persist and keep your anchor lowered, and you sacrifice your comfort to continue looking for a solution because you know you will benefit from the final outcome. Whereas, you lift your anchor when going through a minor issue that does not need any extra worry or pressure. You sit tight and allow things to unfold until the issue passes by without your interference or loss of comfort. Lastly, you cut off your anchor when you have a grudge that is hindering your growth or holding you down from moving ahead in your life. That anchor could be a mistake that you have made in your past, which you are not forgetting, nor are you able to forgive yourself for it. Or it can also be a person who wronged you in the past, and you have some distasteful feelings and even bigger grudge toward them and cannot bring yourself to forgive. Hence, here you should decide to cut your anchor off and move on from those feelings and grudges by forgiving yourself and others. Doing so will bring about more joy and peacefulness into your world.

Not being able to forgive and move on will only affect you negatively in your life. There are so many different emotions and feelings that you can go through, which will only bring about negativity into your life, especially if you are not able to build a strong emotional immunity from going through and experiencing them. Examples of such emotions and feelings are anger, sadness, and at the top of the pyramid is the feeling of being betrayed. Avoid being a prisoner under these feelings and emotions, regardless of the injustice and hopelessness that caused you to harbor those feelings and emotions toward yourself or others.

To better understand the effect of living your life harboring negative feelings and not forgiving yourself and others for past mistakes on your overall mental and physical health, you can try the empty glass experiment. Try holding and raising an empty glass for 20 minutes in the air, and you will notice that after a while, it's going to start feeling like it's full. Eventually, within an hour or two or more, your hand will start shaking. If you continue holding the glass for more than a few hours, your hands will start feeling numb. Hence, it does not matter how empty or full, how heavy or light the weight of that glass is. What matters is how long you are holding onto it. If you hold it for a minute, it's not a problem. If you hold it for an hour, you will have an ache in your arm. If you hold it for a day, your arm will feel numb and paralyzed. In each case, the weight of the glass doesn't change, but the longer you hold it, the heavier it becomes for you. What you can learn from this is that the stress, worries, and grudges in your life are like that empty glass. Those issues, grudges, and worries are more than likely just some empty, hollow issues that you choose to make something out of, and you choose to breathe life into. If you think about those issues and worries for a day, nothing happens. If you think about them all day long, they will begin to hurt. The more you think of them, the more pain, hurt, and paralyzed you will become physically, emotionally, and mentally. So, remember to always put the glass down at least every once and awhile. Additionally, always remember to forgive yourself for the bad choices and decisions, and learn to forgive others who have wronged you for the bad experiences they have put you through. However, never forget the lessons you learned from those past experiences and decisions, and always commit yourself to integrating those lessons learned into your everyday life.

Reasons, tips, and some useful techniques to help you find forgiveness in your heart for yourself and others:

- Start with forgiving yourself for things you did or did not do in your past. Live in the present, and remember that the more you hold onto grudges and conflicts, the more they will affect your life negatively.

- Change your views and interpretations of issues or experiences you have faced in your past, and take them as a necessary thing for growing and maturing.

- Understand that no one is perfect and that everyone will eventually make a big or a small mistake in their life. On the other hand, never shy away from making mistakes or bad decisions in your life. You will always learn and grasp the lessons and morals of those decisions and experiences better when you go through them, regardless of whether it was a good or a bad decision or experience.

- Master the art of looking into issues in your life with a bird's-eye view to see the whole picture from all its angles, and realize that nothing is bigger than life, not you, and not your past issues and grudges.

- Meditate and commit yourself to govern your emotions and learn to control your anger instead of allowing your anger to control you.

- Put yourself in the other person's shoes and view the issue from their point of view to understand why they did what they did.

- Gauge what and how much the other person affected you, and remember that no matter how they wronged you, you still benefited from their actions. They have knowingly put you through an experience that taught you a new lesson, which will help in navigating your life moving forward.

CHAPTER FIVE

Building friendships on a solid ground of trust

"

Friendship is a pure love without any underlying motives or hidden desires.

Every authentic friendship between two or more people is built on caring for and trusting each other. If your friendship lacks any of these two elements, then you will find it difficult to maintain that friendship, because once the acts of caring and trusting each other cease to exist, there is no difference between staying in or leaving that friendship. A friend should be as important and dear to you as your real brother or sister, if not more. They should never be an afterthought. In life, a friend can easily be closer to you than your real brother or sister, and he or she can reach that higher place in your world for many reasons. At the top of those reasons is the fact that you cannot choose your siblings in life. However, you can choose your friends, and you can decide to call him or her a brother or a sister, and you can choose them to be in your inner family circle. Certainly, being able to choose your friends will not stop you from making bad choices. You can always still make the mistake of holding into things and people because they are either expensive or flashy. Sometimes you will go as far as thinking that you cannot live without their existence in your life. Of course, that's one of the biggest mistakes you can make in life because the truth is that the worth of an object or a person is not in how expensive or flashy, they are, but rather the worth is in your need for them to exist in your life. The more you need them in your life, the worthier they are to you.

Be cautious and don't be quick in judging others, because your heart and mind sometimes trick you into feeling and seeing things that are not real. When making an important decision as giving your trust to another person, you should try to strike a balance between using your heart and mind while making that decision. Doing that will give you a better chance of finding friends that you can give your trust to. Additionally, the sole reason for you to find someone and then call them your friends is because you care for and trust them. However, within that trust lies so many different and important aspects and characteristics. You trust that you can confide in them and share your secrets, troubles, happiness, or joy without the fear of being betrayed. You call them your friends, and you give them your trust because they can see things in you even while you are trying to hide them from everyone. They see the sadness hiding behind your smile and the pain within your eyes. They see your good intentions behind your actions without you explaining anything. You befriend them because they see your kindness behind your anger, they feel your strength behind your crying, and they grasp the logic in your silence.

You can look and wish for a real friendship, but to actually come by and cultivate a real friendship, a wishful thinking to find a good friend will not suffice. Instead, a whole lifetime will be required to be able to solidify and battle-test that friendship. Real friendship is like a seed that requires a long time to grow and requires even more attention to flourish. Authentic friendships are not easy to come by, and sometimes you will need to build a wall around you and live in isolation, not to be far away from others, but rather to see who's going to break that wall to see and be with you. To recognize a real friendship, you will need to have it battle-tested, and you need it to go through all the good and bad times and it must come out even stronger than it ever was. You will recognize that your friendship is real when you acknowledge that it's impossible to leave out or remove your friends from your life. Your friendship is real when you know that it's impossible to forget your friends, whether alive or dead. You know that your friends are real when they don't mind sharing their opinions about something or someone in your life regardless of how unpopular that opinion is going to be with you. They stay truthful with you, not because they want to hurt you or deter you from something good, but rather their only purpose is to be your reality check and because they care about your wellbeing and success. You know they are real and sincere with you not because they are there to cheer you up when you succeed, rather it's because they are there for you when you fail and when you need a hand to pick you up and support you through your hardest times.

You should always be able to openly share your opinions or advice with your closest friends regardless of whether those opinions or advice are about them or others, and regardless of whether they will like them or not. Professing your opinions and advice to your friends, especially if they don't agree with it or like it, can affect your friendship negatively regardless of how strong that relationship is. However, the key here is that it's okay for your opinions and advice to affect your friendship temporarily, be it with intense arguments or disagreements. Still, you should never allow them to affect it permanently. Hence, you can and should always try to protect that friendship by professing your opinion without sounding negative and by delivering your advice without passing judgment to the person on the receiving end. For your opinion or advice to be received properly, two of the most important prerequisites that need to exist are circumstance and timing of delivery. Therefore, you will need to learn how to pick and choose your moments because the acceptance of that opinion or advice will largely depend not only on the timing of the delivery but also the method by which you deliver your opinion. It will take you years of life experiences and probably some verbal and nonverbal fights to reach a level where you can control your emotions and master an even-keeled tone for delivering your advice and opinions. Your opinion and advice must come from a pure heart without malice or any malicious intent or desire, and certainly not for any personal gain. Being the sole beneficiary of your friend' heeding your advice is the only time that you should never advise your friend because it will taint your friendship, and you will lose your friend's trust.

Trust is a delicate entity that must be built on a solid and clear ground of understanding each other's motives. It must be surrounded by and protected using honesty and communication between all parties involved. In life, two reasons prevent you from placing your trust in a person. The first would be because you don't know them, and the second would be because you truly know them, and so you recognize that you cannot trust them. However, knowledge is different than understanding, and you can achieve one without achieving the other. You can know someone but can never understand them, and you can also understand someone without knowing them. So, before calling someone a friend and placing your trust in them, make sure to know them and understand their motive for befriending you. You should always take precautions before befriending someone and opening yourself or placing your trust in them. You do that for you not to lose trust in people but to protect yourself from being hurt as well.

For your friendship to last, don't build it on expectations and just let it be. Allow it to go through the ups and downs and let it grow organically and without any constraint or pressure. Friendship is not always a balanced arrangement; it's not always about giving and taking in equal shares. Rather, it's grounded on a feeling that you know who will be there for you, not only during your success and happiness but in your time of failures and grief as well. Expectation can ruin your friendships. So, you should try your hardest to avoid falling into the expectation's trap and try to restore any friendship you ended because of it. Remember that you are not a perfect human being, and neither are your friends, so don't expect them to be perfect. Accept who and what they are while making sure they don't expect you to be perfect, and they should also accept who and what you are.

Friends will have a lot of influence when it comes to affecting your life direction and decisions while you are working on building and molding your character. By interacting with your friends and going through a mix of good and bad experiences with them, you gain so many different life skills and lessons, which in turn help you in navigating through anything that life throws at you. While going through life, you will meet and befriend so many different types of people, each with their aspirations and ambitions. Some of your friends can help you set your life priorities and give you a different point of view or take on life. Some can hold you accountable for your actions and can give you a reality check every now and then. Others can support you and stand by you through thick and thin, while others can hurt you and betray the confidence and trust you gave them. To flourish and to achieve your goal to be happier, you need to make sure to hold on tightly to those friends who will help you in clarifying your priorities. You will need to restore your friendships with those who are not perfect and always get under your skin but yet keep giving you reality checks and holding you accountable for your actions.

Lastly, with all the technology and social media platforms in the world, you may see that the number of people you call friends increased, but their loyalty decreased. You can always get betrayed by someone you called a friend at some point in time. Yet, most of the time, the betrayal itself will not hurt you, but finding out the person who betrayed you may kill you. Hence, make sure to utilize your trust wisely and never go in life looking for a hundred friends, but rather try to look for one friend for a hundred years. Don't shy away from unfriending and cutting your ties with those who betray your trust, because a friend you can't trust is no friend. Understand that some people come into your life as a lesson while others come into it as a blessing. So, make sure to learn from the lessons while appreciating and being thankful for the blessings.

Some characteristics and qualities to look for when befriending someone, alongside some methods to cultivate an everlasting, pure friendship:

- Look for people who are trustworthy and decent, for when you share your secrets with them or show your true feelings and emotions to them, you will feel safe in doing so.

- Befriend people who are dependable when you need them to be, and fun and silly all the other times. A friendship that doesn't bring you joy, wholeness, and happiness is better dead than alive.

- Your friends should be supportive in all the good and bad times because a hand that helps you stand up when you fall is better than a thousand that shake your hand when you arrive at the finish line. Look for that hand that comes to your aid when you fall, and stay away from a hand that only shows up when you succeed and arrive at the finish line.

- Surround yourself with friends who are nonjudgmental toward you when you are being yourself, but judgmental and confrontational when you mess up and need someone to straighten you out and point out your mistakes for you to learn from.

- Be aware of allowing these people to come into your life: a person who wrongs you but will wait for you to apologize, or a person you ignored their misdeeds against you and they thought you were dumb or afraid for not reacting.

- Learn to strike a balance between when to give out your opinions and when and how much advice you should give to your friends because giving advice is like giving medicine: a small dose at a time will cure, but a bigger dose all at once may kill.

- Avoid being a person who ignores his or her own transgressions and can only see other's wrongs.

- Your friends' hearts are like an ocean, and your friendship with them is like a ship sailing in it, so be careful when you poke a hole in your friendships and the trust between you because an ocean won't support a ship with a hole in it.

- If you have two eyes, then don't treat people with your ears! Treat people with what you see from them, not what you hear about them.

CHAPTER SIX

Becoming a happy kid again

> **"**
>
> A happy person is nothing more than a person bringing out
> the kid living within them.

What is happiness, and who can attain it, and how can one achieve it?

There is not one thing in this world that will bring you happiness. Thus, there is no universal definition for happiness because happiness requires a combination of so many different things, and it comes in so many various forms, shapes, and sizes. Therefore, each person has his or her way of defining happiness. Happiness is not something you can gain or lose in a few hours, like pleasurable sensations such as consuming food for some people or making money for others. Happiness is an end or a goal that encompasses the totality of your life. Happiness is the ultimate value of your life as lived up to this moment, measuring how well you have lived up to your full potential as a human being. You must realize that there is no such thing as an ultimate, final, and complete happiness that you can achieve, at least not while you are alive. However, there is a state of mind and soul that you can fill with joy and contentment that will overpower and conquer any other mood. Happiness, in all its different forms, shapes, and sizes, can have commonly shared characteristics that are associated with happy people, a happy life, and happy actions. Happiness encompasses knowing your goal and purpose in life, as well as having a state of mind and soul of self-worth, and having the capacity to be content with what you have and what you are. Lastly, it also encompasses being able to find peace within yourself and with others.

People commonly refer to a life without trouble, complications, or sadness, and filled with luxury as a happy life. That type of belief when it comes to happiness is just another corrupt, deceptive illusion-filled belief that is degrading societies across the world. By believing in that illusion-filled happiness and pushing yourself toward that type of state of mind, you are doing yourself more harm than good. You go in life trying to live it stress-free with no sadness and no trouble. Doing so will eventually prevent you from doing anything that might bring you the most happiness, and you end bringing about all the negativity that you were trying to avoid.

You go through life, putting so much pressure on yourself trying to prevent any sadness, stress, or trouble from coming into your life. By doing that, you are unknowingly shackling yourself, your spirit, and soul from growing and maturing in this life. You avoid confronting your boss at work when they make a mistake because you are afraid of getting fired. You avoid getting married because you don't want to lose your independence. You avoid having babies because you don't want to sacrifice your peace of mind. You don't want to follow your dreams because you worry about people's perception of you and your success or failures. You can face some decisions and experiences in life that can affect it minimally or significantly. Yet, by trying to avoid any unwanted tension, stress, heartache, and trouble from seeping into your life, you are depriving yourself of some needed and viable experiences. Those unfavorable experiences can contribute in making and showing the real you. They can push you toward understanding your life purpose and can help you in realizing and finding happiness in every situation.

Happiness is a choice, and you can choose to be happy and achieve a happy state of mind because happiness comes from within. Once you decide that you will be happy, and once you choose to redefine happiness and you decide to enjoy the struggles and the failures as much as you enjoy the fun times and successes, you will be on the right path toward filling your life with happiness. You can only see and appreciate the stars in the darkness; the darker the night, the brighter the stars become. Therefore, you should treat your harsh times with acceptance and resiliency because that's only going to make you shine even more vividly and, consequently, become happier. Yet, to be able to accept your darker times, you will need that light at the end of the tunnel to keep you going, and that light will radiate only by knowing your purpose and goal in life. Therefore, for you, as an adult, to find true happiness, knowing your purpose and goals in life is a must and working on achieving them is a requirement. Your goals and purpose in life are the pillars that will bring about all other aspects of happiness, such as joy, self-worth, peace, and contentment.

Using your gifts

"The meaning of life is to find your gift. The purpose of life is to give it away." Pablo Picasso

You can spend years and years trying to find real happiness, and you might end up hurting yourself in the process. I wish I could tell you that there is an actual store that you can visit whenever you needed to buy some real happiness, but in reality, that store is imaginary and exists only within you. It can be within your brain, heart, soul, or all of the above. You just need to know it, realize it, understand it, and appreciate it. Only then can you put that happiness store to work and use it to improve yourself and better your life.

Happiness is a state of mind which you experienced at some point in your life. You just need to remember how to bring it about into your life again and again. Some people find happiness with their hearts, others with their minds and thoughts, while others find it with their souls and spirits. Yet, we all find happiness by using the gifts, talents, and skills we already possess. If you are an artist, you will probably find more happiness exercising your love of art, be it singing, drawing, writing, or any other form of art that requires you to use your talents, skills, and other gifts you might have. You exercise that form of art and not only be able to find solace and happiness in doing or finishing that song, poem, painting, book, or any other piece of art, but others will also find themselves in that poem, painting, or book through you. They will be inspired to find their happiness through your inspiring journey, which keeps radiating from your art, which you have brought to life. By using and utilizing the talent you have, you were able to help not only yourself but also inspire and help others along the way, which is the ultimate objective to achieve while utilizing your talents and gifts.

You can use an existing tangible talent to fill your life with happiness. On the other hand, you can find happiness utilizing other types of gifts in your life, such as finding and surrounding yourself with the gift of love. There has always been a particular type of joy, laughter, and happiness that you can only find when you surround yourself with those who loves you and those whom you love. Whether those people are your family or friends, just make sure to be with them and be surrounded by them out of love and without any expectations, because expectations will be the downfall, and it will suck all the joy and happiness from it. Love them for whom and what they are expecting nothing but the love and happiness that comes from being with them.

Additionally, you can also find happiness by meditating or praying and observing and enjoying your surroundings. Praying and meditating is some of the few activities that has zero negative side effects, and the more of it you do, the better you become at understanding and controlling your surroundings. The only time your mind, spirit, and soul can take an actual break from the hectic life around you is by exercising either of the above practices. By silencing the world around you and focusing on your internal self, you allow yourself to feel the emptiness of the space surrounding it and for your consciousness to be in harmony with the world you strive toward. Usually, any action that causes you to lose your sense of time can relieve you of any physical, emotional stress and fatigue, which will eventually lead you to the temporary state of mind you call happiness. No matter the method by which you find happiness, you just need to realize that happiness, its meaning, and how you can bring it about into your life, will always be objective and depend on you as a person and your maturity and circumstances.

Giving more and asking for less

You might think happiness will come about once you get what you desire in life, such as money, luxury, sex, or food. However, what you need to know is that you don't achieve happiness by satisfying your desires rather by being able to limit them. You do it by focusing on that which fulfills your happiness and which pushes you toward achieving your purpose and goals. A common characteristic that all humans have is greed, in that, the more they get, the more they want. Yet, people come closer to finding and creating happiness not by seeking more but by evolving and learning to enjoy living with less. The core of happiness is more about giving-out than it is about taking in. Giving out, be it tangible and physical, such as money, food, and other goods, or intangible and spiritual such as love, hope, and inspiration, is the single action that will bring you closer to your ultimate happiness. Once you can give more in life than you take, you will understand that you are as close to your ultimate happiness as you are ever going to be. You will realize that you are only able to give more because you have more of that which you are giving. In life, you cannot give out what you don't have. You cannot give out food without having it, and you cannot give out love and hope without having it yourself. Learn that your happiness will only grow when you share it with others, and the more happiness you give to others, the more you will have of it for yourself. That dream of being rich tangibly or intangibly will eventually materialize when you start giving out more of what you already have. Try giving out non-tangible and non-material items that are at your disposal, and that won't cost you a thing to give. Change your life around by giving out more kindness and smiles and more compassion and love. Start with your own family and relatives, and eventually, give out more of that to the world around you. Ask for less and give more, because the act of giving while making sure to live in the present is more fulfilling and rewarding than asking for more and worrying about the future.

Living in the present

You go through life working, studying, hustling, being patient, and showing resiliency. Within your busy life, you either forget or intentionally postpone enjoying your life, thinking that you will eventually have that time. Ask yourself, what is it that you dream of doing or aspire to do when you have that magical time you are waiting for to come into your life? Now go ahead and jot down five of the things that you aspire to do once that magical time arrives.

1.

2.

3.

4.

5.

I can tell you that you can already do at least three out of the five things you listed above. You can do them now, and without waiting for a future time or future date. You don't have to, and you shouldn't have to wait for your retirement or for when your kids grow up if you have any, for you to have that magical free time to start enjoying life. What guarantees do you have that you will be better off postponing enjoying your life physically, mentally, or spiritually? What assurances do you have that are making you postpone doing all the things that you aspire to do until your retirement or until that future magical date and time comes around? When that future time and date comes around, you might not be able to do one or many of the items you listed above, and there is a chance that you might not even live to see that day come. Therefore, you just need to learn how to live in the present. Focus on enjoying your life with what you have and who you are now. Understand that you have no power over your past. Realize that what happened in your past has already happened, and there is no going back in time. The more you focus on living in the past, the more you bring hurt, displeasure, and depression into your present life. Thus, the only thing you can do with your past is to learn from it and use it to improve yourself and to move forward in your life.

While you shouldn't live in your past, you shouldn't live in your future either. Living in the future will bring you nothing but anxiety and despair, and it will cripple you from enjoying your life and your present time. You need to be able to plan for the future and see your plan materialize without losing grasp of your present time. Learn to recognize the fine line that exists between planning your future and getting lost in it. Commit yourself to living in the present and making peace with yourself as well as with others, and recognize that whatever you do in the present will wipe out your past and will determine and shape your future. So, make sure to live in the present while focusing on training yourself and especially your mind to be present and aware of each and every present moment. Doing that will make it easier for you to be happy, and it will lift your spirit and life. Then and only then you will have a holistic view of your life and your happiness.

Rediscovering your inner child

Kids are evil. They are evil, not literally but because they can make every living adult jealous of the happiness they have and the happiness they show in their lives, requiring little to nothing. You stop at a stoplight, and you see kids holding their parents' hands and hopping around full of joy while crossing the street. You go to a park and see kids throwing their clothes off and running and jumping around and playing in the fountain water without even caring about their surroundings. All they see is water and fountain, and in their minds, it means running and getting wet and having fun. You go to the beach, and I dare you to see any kid sitting in the sand with their clothes on because they think that they don't look good with their clothes off or that their body is not beach-ready. You give a kid a cookie, and even though those little monsters might ask for more cookies, they will still be mighty happy with the cookie they already have, and they will tear that cookie apart eating it. It's easier for kids to unearth the happiness within them because of their young age and lack of life experiences. Their young age and lack of life experiences allow them to hold on to a pure heart and mind that's yet to be poisoned by the adult greed, hate, and lack of purpose and lack of self-worth. On top of that, kids don't care or give an F about what anyone thinks of them. They reach heights of happiness higher than any adult, young adult, mature, or old could ever achieve. Alongside having a pure heart and mind and all the other reasons listed above that allow kids to display the happiness that they have is the way their mind and memory function.

Kids' memories and minds work magically, in that they can move on or forget about having a bad day within an hour of having a good time. That's because they are only living in and thinking about the present, not the past nor the future. That's not the case when it comes to anyone who is not in that carefree phase, as those people tend to be either depressed or anxious. They are depressed because they are stuck living in the past or anxious because they are afraid of the future. One thing you can learn from these kids is that rediscovering your inner child does not mean being reckless or irresponsible. Instead, it means living your life in the present and trying to unearth the happiness that exists within you while making sure to bring out your inner child without being self-conscious and without caring about what others would think of you.

In life, you grow older not because you stopped loving all you used to do when you were a child, or because you stopped loving those cookies or candies you loved when you were a child. Nor is it because you stopped loving the games or the TV shows you used to enjoy playing or watching when you were a child. Instead, it's because you stopped doing all that you loved, and you convinced yourself that you have to stop doing some if not all that you used to enjoy when you were a child for you to become an adult, and to allow yourself to grow older and mature. Hence, it's going to require a decision and some convincing from within that you can do some if not all that you used to love doing when you were a child so that you can find your inner child and inject some peace, love, and happiness back into your life again. You will need to remind yourself of how to live your life in the present and how to bring about that carefree zone back into your life. Lastly, you will need to commit yourself to working on purifying your heart and mind from all the corruption and abuse that life drove into them.

Some methods and techniques to finding happiness:

- Choose happiness and learn how to handle and live with all the pressure and issues in your life.

- Stop worrying and lamenting about your past and future and live in your present.

- Aspire to give more and take less.

- Find your passion and live with it and by it and never lose sight of it.

- Surround yourself with loved ones and friends.

- Love yourself and work on understanding your self-worth.

- Find your inner child and stop putting too much weight on other people's opinions of you. If you see a fountain in the park, do what any other kid would do and get naked and walk into that fountain. However, even though doing that would be fun and funny to see at the same time, I hope you don't really do it because most likely, it is illegal, especially for adults, and you will end up in jail. But you get the idea, which is to free yourself from other people's opinions and start enjoying your life carefree.

CHAPTER SEVEN

Finding a purpose and forming peace with yourself

"

Control, purpose, and experiences are your building blocks
for achieving a peaceful life.

For you to move ahead in life and to find and bring happiness
about into your life, making peace with yourself, as well as with
others around you, is one of the stepping stones toward
achieving that goal. Reaching peace with self requires a
significant level of control over your mind, heart, and emotions.
Having that control will, in turn, allow you to maintain the ability
to process your life and your interactions with others as is and
not as you think it should or ought to be. The ability to control
your mind and emotions will help you in moving forward in life
regardless of the mistakes and wrongdoings of yourself and
others against you. It will encourage you to live your life in the
present, and it will give you the power to forgive yourself as
well as others' mistakes, blunders, and slip-ups. Learning to
control your mind and emotion allows you to forgive yourself
for past mistakes and gives you the ability to manage any hate

that might exist within your heart for all the wrongdoings from yourself and others toward yourself.

Additionally, reaching peace with yourself requires an extraordinary level of faith and acceptance of yourself and your own life. It will start by accepting who and what you are and what you are not, then moving on to learning to accept others for what and who they are. Teaching yourself the trait of acceptance will, in turn, allow you to receive and embrace the good and the bad in life and of the people living in it. It will give you the needed energy, and it will push you toward achieving peace with self and, consequently, with others.

Find and make peace with yourself before trying to make peace with others

Finding peace and making peace with others is a noble idea that is accessible to all. Yet, because of the level of difficulty in accomplishing it, only a few people can and will ever be able to realize and achieve it. The challenge in making peace with others lies in all the preconditions that come before it, prerequisites such as making peace with one's self. Finding peace with self is the ultimate peace because, without it, you will never find peace in life. Reaching peace with self encompasses knowing who you are as a person and knowing what and who is essential for and within your life. You shouldn't expect that you will just stumble upon finding who and what you are because finding one's self on its own is not an easy task. A lot of people will go through life and will keep on struggling to know who they are, and they will also find a hard time understanding what's important in their lives. Therefore, when you decide to take on that journey and as you go through life, you will find that there are many ways, methods, and paths that will help you in knowing who you are and what is essential in your life. Examples of such techniques are meditation, soul-searching, and encountering some extreme life experiences such as life or death. All these methods and experiences will help in opening a window into your identity and the person living within you. Then and only then, you might have a better chance of achieving peace with yourself.

For you to go through life, you will need to nourish and feed your body with the nutrition and elements it needs to function and perform its daily chore and physical activities. For your body to be healthy, a minimum amount of physical activity is required to keep all the muscles, joints, organs functioning properly. Likewise, for your mind to function properly and to stay sharp and for you to better understand yourself and to have a chance at finding peace with yourself, a minimum amount of meditation, experiences, and soul-searching are required. Additionally, for your soul to be content and never get lost in the hectic life you go through, you will need to find your purpose and passion in life. Utilizing meditation, soul-searching, or extreme life experiences, or a combination of all the above will help you in doing just that.

Meditation

Meditation is one of the main exercises or methods that will help you find and know who you are. It will help you in finding that which is vital in your life. Meditation will help you to achieve that, because one of the most important aspects of meditation is the fact that it will provide you with the time needed to connect with yourself, and it will allow you to focus on finding your inner self. Meditation combines so many different exercises, such as mindfulness meditation, breath awareness meditation, kundalini yoga, and transcendental meditation, all of which will help you in training and calming the mind and aid you in finding a sense of inner harmony. Each one of these exercises has its benefits. Yet, they all share some common benefits such as relaxation of the mind and body, free of any tension or emotional strain, and liberation of the mind from attachment to things it cannot control, be it external circumstances or internal emotions. All meditation exercises help in relaxing and liberating the mind, and for you to achieve peace with self and peace with others, you should focus on mindfulness meditation. By doing mindfulness meditation, you develop a strong, inner balance and an even better understanding of what is going on inside your head. This exercise will help you in observing your feelings and thoughts as they jump around in your mind, and it will help you in understanding their pattern and association, be it pleasant or unpleasant, good or bad. Once you do a few mindfulness exercises, you will start having more control over your thoughts and emotions while having less tension and attachment to things you cannot control.

Soul-searching

Soul-searching and finding your purpose in life will lead you to have peace with yourself. Certainly, it will be hard for you to find peace with yourself without discovering and realizing that thing, that passion which stirs your inner fire and keeps you going in life. Your purpose is directly related to your passion, and it's tightly correlated to what motivates you, and to that which makes you want to take action in life. It does not matter how big or small the thing that stirs your fire and passion, and it does not have to be a life- or world-changing thing. Instead, it just needs to matter to you and only you. It can be as big as making a difference in the community you live in, or it can also be as small as making a positive difference with a single family member. Keep searching and researching until you find the one thing you have always wanted and talked about doing but never did. You might struggle to find that one thing, but you should never quit, and you should try taking it even further and looking for the thing you wanted to get or buy for yourself, or the place you wanted to visit or live in before you leave this world. Once you find your purpose or goals in life, you can start by getting rid of the things, obstacles, habits, or people who are preventing you from pursuing or achieving them. Additionally, to keep on pursuing your purpose and passion in life and to take a huge step forward in finding peace with yourself, you need to make sure to surround yourself with people who inspire you to find and hold tight to your passion and purpose in life. Furthermore, you will need those people in your life because they will support and push you to keep on going and to keep persisting no matter what obstacles you are facing.

Encountering extreme life experiences such as life or death

One last element that will help you in your quest toward achieving peace with yourself is encountering some extreme life experiences such as life or death or both. In life, most of the time, you cannot change a person's life just by giving them advice, and that's mainly because giving and receiving advice is very often just less productive and effective than what some people believe. The impact of advice is affected by so many variables. Sometimes it's the methods and knowledge of the person giving advice. Other times it's the willingness and openness of the person receiving advice. Whereas, experiences, painful or not, are more valuable than advice because they will resonate more due to the emotional journey that those life experiences demand. You will learn more from the emotional journey during those life experiences than from receiving advice and trying to apply it to your own experience. Pain, be it physical, mental, or emotional, will teach you more about yourself than any advice you will ever receive. As you go through different life experiences, you gain a combination of physical and mental strength, which aids and guides you through your upcoming challenges and experiences. For example, in most cases, you do not need to lose someone you love or something valuable for you to comprehend or realize how important those people or things in your life are. Yet, going through a personal loss will undoubtedly make you understand all that's important in your life. It will allow you to let go of things hanging over your heart and mind. You can always try to mimic those extreme life experiences such as death by visiting a cemetery or a loved one's grave while the sun is out, of course, because visiting at night will probably put you in a grave yourself. Visiting a cemetery will help you put your life in perspective and will allow you to see the world using different lenses. Additionally, you can also experience the opposite end of the spectrum and experience a new life by going through the experience of having a newborn baby. The experience of having a baby or giving birth to one is one of the most life-changing, insightful experiences a person can go through. Thus, by spending some time examining your own experience in visiting a cemetery, a newborn, or any other experience in life, you gain a better understanding of yourself and a more holistic view of your surroundings. Eventually, you become better at differentiating what is essential in your life and what things you would be better letting go of to optimize yourself, your living, and, consequently, become a better you.

Once you know who you are, your true purpose, and you are able to accept and embrace your true identity, then and only then can you reach that pinnacle of having peace with yourself. Reaching and achieving peace with yourself will open up so many doors and new opportunities for you and your life will take a sharp turn for the better. You will start enjoying the advantages and benefits of finding peace with yourself, advantages such as learning to forgive and letting go of things anchoring you down, less physical and mental stress and diseases, more self-worth and happiness, and more control over your life. Lastly, by going through all those life experiences from meditation to soul-searching, extreme life experiences, and by digging deep into yourself, knowing and understanding, you ultimately will be able to achieve peace with others.

Some tips to help you find peace and form peace with yourself and others:

- Try to have an eye that only sees and looks for the beauty in people and other things in life. Teach your heart to forgive the worst and to accept the bad before the good. Allow your mind to only think of and aspire to the best, and fill your soul with hope and ambition.

- Learn and understand yourself and try to find your calling and purpose in life, for it will propel you into making peace with yourself. The more you work toward achieving your calling in life, the closer you will be to finding and making peace with yourself and, consequently, with others.

- Teach yourself to let go of things bringing you down, especially the things that you have control over. Use all the methods discussed above, be it meditation in all its forms, soul-searching, or going through extreme life experiences to master and hone your control over yourself and your life.

- Embrace your painful experiences, and make sure never to forget them but rather try to forgive them and learn from them and use them to push forward by loving yourself and others.

- Look at your toughest issues and challenges as golden opportunities for you to exercise and strengthen every mental aspect that you lack when you face hard times. It can be patience, emotional control, or anger management. Yet, regardless of the characteristic strength, you are lacking, as you go through the different types of experiences, just make sure to come out from it stronger and having learned or fixed something about life or yourself.

PART TWO

Understanding your world

CHAPTER EIGHT

Embracing your world and finding its perfection

"

A perfect world exists, it can't be seen, but it can be felt,

understood, and embraced.

A perfect world existence is one of the most interesting and exciting life and philosophical topics and questions which keeps you and everybody else busy searching for and aspiring to achieve. It combines so many different ideologies, concepts, philosophies, and theories under it, including religion, logic, and science. You don't have to see something to believe in its existence; you only need to study it and contemplate it to realize its existence or not. Therefore, a perfect world does exist, be it in religion, logic, and even science. When it comes to logic, no two humans will have the same definition or meaning of what it means to be perfect or to live in a perfect world. The meaning of being perfect or of living in a perfect world will change from one person to another. As long as people mature and change throughout life with its ups and downs, their meaning of perfect will change as well.

On the other hand, most known religions in this world agree on the concept of one world with a God or gods who are all-knowing and all-powerful, and therefore this world is perfect because a perfect entity created it. Additionally, many scientific clues steer us into seeing this world as self-healing and self-ruling from the smallest grains of sand, the oceans, to all the other planets and space around it and far beyond. Therefore, this world is perfect. You, as well as others, can envision and strive for a perfect world based on your own visions and plans. God created a perfect world. The world you live in is self-healing, self-ruling. The world you live in is expandable, flexible, and versatile. Therefore, this world is perfect.

Religion

"The world is created by a perfect entity, and therefore, this world is perfect because a perfect entity will only create a perfect world. God created a perfect world."

When considering the common definition of the adjective, "perfect" which encompasses all the required or desirable elements, qualities, and characteristics, and being as good as it is possible to be, you can state that the creator of this world has created a perfect world. This world is perfect for humans as well as other living organisms to live and inhabit, and search and research, and evolve as a unit. The atmosphere and all the microorganisms that live within this world are under one ecosystem, which, if you spend more time studying, you will eventually be able to answer a lot of the questions about the ways and methods of coexisting and living with the world around you. You will ultimately match this perfect world you inhabit. The way humans use their logic and how they process the knowledge they have is the main reason they are still not able to reach the optimal way of life that would allow them to live in a perfect way and in a harmony that matches this perfect world. God gave humans all the tools and capabilities to reach that perfect state of mind and to reach that state of perfection in all aspects of their lives. Yet, humans choose not to utilize those tools and capabilities that God blessed them with. Humans want a perfect world, but they either don't use and improve the skills they have to reach or better yet sustain a perfect world in which they already inhabit. Or they lack the mental powers, the required compassion, as well as the scientific knowledge altogether, to which the perfect world will adhere to.

In life, there is a certain level of knowledge, mental capacity, and compassion required for every job, task, and aspect of life for that task or job to be accomplished and sustained. Hence, reaching a perfect life or an ideal world is not an easy task and requires the ultimate level of knowledge, mental capacities, and compassion. Moreover, humans do have their God-given potential and capabilities, which holds the secret recipe for finding and building a perfect world. Still, they don't own the key or "knowledge" to unlock those capabilities. However, it's not a surprise that humans lack the knowledge to unlock those capabilities. It makes total sense because it's just part of their evolution. The process of evolution and maturing as we know it comes in stages, and the knowledge to unlock those capabilities is part of human evolution, which also comes in stages. Humans judging this world as not perfect are basically either jumping through stages and chapters of the evolutionary process or confusing the world ecosystem perfection with their humanmade world surrounding them. Again, a perfect world varies from a person to another, and a person's surrounding imperfections does not mean that the world as a whole is imperfect.

Science

"The world we live in is expandable, flexible, versatile, self-healing, and self-ruling."

The world you live in is a self-fixing, self-healing world. The world you live in is perfect because when talking about the world you live in as a single object (planet earth as an example), you can state that this world is expanding and shrinking, progressing and regressing as humans progress and regress. Much scientific research and multiple theories have studied the world self-healing phenomenon and provided some serious arguments and proofs for it. Those arguments were so convincing to the point where leading world countries started taking those arguments into account and started applying methods and procedures to their way of life to allow the earth to heal and recover on its own. On the other hand, humans are an essential part of the world cycle, and they contribute significantly to making this world a good or a bad place. Moreover, advanced comprehension and the ability to use logic are the foundation of their existence. In addition to advanced comprehension and logic, exist the power of free will and the ability of decision making as well. Those features combined are the things that differentiate humans from other living organisms because other organisms either do not have or have in a limited capacity. With the power of free will and the ability to make decisions, humans can build, destroy, and do good or evil. Humans have the ability to achieve a perfect life or world. They just need to choose and strive for a perfect world using their free will.

In your daily life, you can observe examples of self-healing entities such as the earth you inhabit as well as yourself as a human being. The earth's self-healing and self-correcting phenomena have been big topics in the scientific field, and many studies have shown the earth's ability to adjust, evolve, and heal itself. As for humans, they also have a complex self-healing, self-correcting system and mechanism, in which a person breaks a hand, and the body eventually heals itself. With enough time and proper care, the hand will, in most cases, return to its original form and function. Moreover, when a person makes a painful mistake, he or she will try to avoid repeating the same mistake the next time they face a similar situation. Hence, these self-healing and self-correcting examples, be it physical or mental, are just some simple instances of the perfections that exist within you and the perfection which surrounds your world.

Logic

"Everyone dreams of a perfect world, but no two can agree on what is a perfect world."

Your perfect world and what you consider to be the optimal way of life and living is not what others may see as a perfect life or a perfect world for themselves. You can envision your perfect world and strive to achieve it. However, for that vision to materialize, and for you to achieve and realize that perfect world you envisioned, you need to prevent yourself from trying to enforce and impose your vision of a perfect world onto others and onto the world around you. Your methods and techniques of achieving and reaching your perfect world are flawed and corrupt. Meaning, it's a mistake for you to think that the world you live in with the people in it are just objects you can control like a video game, moving one piece to a different location whenever you want and your desire or vision change. You need to redefine your understanding and your vision of a perfect world, and you need to make it more inclusive, to account for the world and others living in it, as actual beings with their own desires and wills. Only then can you recalibrate and reassess your vision of a perfect world while making sure to account for all the other moving parts which you cannot control. Then you will learn to live with them and through their choices and transgressions against your perfect world.

So many people in this world die because they judge life as not worth living. While others are foolishly and naively getting killed for ideas and illusions that give them a reason for living.

Therefore, understanding whether living life, even if it's not perfect, is worth it or not, is at the heart of existence. Judging life as not worth living is not a flaw in the world. Rather, it's a flaw in the judgment and knowledge of the person when he/she made that flawed judgement. It's a flaw in judgment because making that decision requires a deeper knowledge and a deeper understanding of the world you live in and the world you desire to live in. You have the ability and will to decide not to live in the world that was given to you. Instead, you can choose the world you have always fantasized about and aspired to live in.

The world you live in is expandable, flexible, and versatile, which means that your world can grow and progress, or shrink and regress, as you grow and progress or shrink and regress. Growing and progressing does not mean gaining more physical mass or getting older. Instead, it means growing and progressing mentally and emotionally. Growing mentally and gaining more knowledge by studying, reading, observing, questioning, and researching will help you understand your own life, and surroundings better. Whereas, progressing and advancing emotionally by meditating, praying, self-observing, and finding an inner peace will help you with connecting better and becoming more compassionate toward life, the world, and your surroundings.

These two acts of developing yourself mentally and emotionally will expand your world and imagination, which in turn will give you a better understanding of your existence. It will illustrate and show your purpose in life. Understanding your purpose in life and finding that which drives you to evolve and thrive for a better life for yourself and others will allow you to reach self-peace, compassion, and satisfaction. Knowing your purpose and realizing that your world has expanded and developed into something way more significant than that which you started with will propels you into reaching that state of self-peace. With all that as a premise, you can define your ideas of a perfect world and work and strive to reach a mental state of mind where you can achieve that perfect world you imagined and dreamed of and obtain physically all that satisfies your vision of a perfect world.

All the moving parts and living organisms that constitute this world, the order, flow, cycle, and complex processes that go into each of the building blocks of this world, including humans, are just some simple examples of the perfection that surrounds this world. With all the knowledge and science humans achieved so far, they are all nothing but a drop in the ocean. Many areas of this world are left unexplored, from the deep ocean to space, from the human brain to the human soul. These unexplored areas will be eventually explored and studied as humans keep their pace of thriving and evolving, which hopefully will allow for a better and wholesome world for you as well as for others.

Therefore, this world is perfect.

A perfect world is a variable world that changes with the person judging or evaluating that world. There is no such thing as a universal meaning for the words "perfect" or "fair" or "just." These adjectives are all variables, and their meanings will change, sometimes drastically, based on the person, community, environment, culture, and beliefs. There are many outside agents that factor in when it comes to defining or describing a perfect entity. Examples of such factors include but are not limited to social norms and pressures, religious guidance and guidelines, instincts, fear, and drugs. All the ones listed and many others not listed can contribute into making and forming that definition or facade of what is considered perfect.

Your background, your upbringing, who brought you up, and the morals and beliefs engraved into your psyche, are all factors that affect the way you act and the method in which you make decisions. This world that you live in is a perfect world because of the self-healing, self-ruling ecosystem that the creator encompassed this world with. The more humans evolve as an organism in all aspects of their lives, mentally or scientifically, and with more compassion for the world they live in, the more this world expands, progresses, and evolves to the extent of perfection because perfection is a variable and an evolving process.

Some tips to reach and realize your perfect world:

- In order to realize a perfect world, you need to believe in its existence, and for you to believe in its existence, you need to modify your understanding of it and to make it inclusive of others.

- Embrace the existence of others, including all of their actions and transcreations within your perfect world. Even though it's your own perfect world, you still need to realize your lack of control over their existence in it.

- Plan your vision and work on realizing it while making sure to stay fluid and open to reassessing the plans, and if needed, choose different routes along the way.

CHAPTER NINE

Aspiring for fairness and fighting for justice

"

> If you can feel pain, then you are alive, and if you can feel other people's pain, then you are a human. But if you can help in soothing others pain, then you are a great being. Once you put them all together, you become alive human being.

Is this world fair and just?

Both principles of fairness and justice are commonly used interchangeably, although they both have some major differences in their meanings and within their applications. In fact, justice is one important part of fairness and can exist without the need for equality. In contrast, when it comes to reaching ultimate and complete fairness, equality is a requirement for it to exist and materialize. Therefore, you need to understand that justice is a means to an end. The end is meant to be complete and principled fairness built on all the justice in this world. Therefore, for you to reach that ultimate fairness, you will need to take a ride on the road of justice.

What if, when someone hurts you physically or emotionally, they get hurt the same way as well? When someone steals from you, someone steals from them too. What if no natural disasters or diseases existed in this world? Will any of the above statements prove the existence of a just world?

The idea that most people have of a "just world" or "justice" is unattainable and, most of the time, misguided and controlled by corrupt beliefs and self-serving emotions and interests. Since the day you were born, you are constantly disciplined and taught by your parents at home and teachers at school that the better you behave, the more reward you get. The harder you work and study, the more reward and better grades you get. So, you are being taught that the idea of justice is all about hard work and being morally good. Only then will you be able to receive all the justice and good in this world. Certainly, this characterization of justice only works with your parents, specifically when you are still at a young age. It works not because they are aiming to be just and fair with you. They are not trying to reward you whenever you are being good or doing a good deed, but rather because they are trying to raise a child and trying to instill some good moral traits into you. Giving you candy and rewarding you is the only way they could control a maniac like you. Moreover, your parents' justice will eventually match life's justice as well, and you will notice that your parents will start acting and unjustly reacting toward you, at least according to you and your justice gauge. This idea that hardworking people, as well as morally good people, will be rewarded more in life is just a misguided belief and wishful thinking by delusional people. I am not telling you that you should stop working hard or being morally good to start living in a just world. Especially if you believe in the existence of the afterlife, you should definitely try to be morally good. However, I am just saying that you need to fix and modify your definition and understanding of a just world. Whether you are morally good and a hardworking person or not, you need to suck it up and understand that life's fairness is not about what life gives or takes from you. Rather, it's about what you get and take for yourself.

A teacher receives less than a football player, and a cancer doctor or researcher receives less than a musician. Both the doctor and teacher work as hard if not more than the football player or the musician, and they are as good in their fields as the other two. Yet, they both make considerably less than the football player or the musician. Certainly, this is no knock-on athletes or musicians and artists, because sports and art do save lives in their own ways, and a community with no art or artists is a lifeless one. However, we can deduce that life's justice, and fairness is not about working harder, nor is it about being morally good. On the contrary, in life, more often than not, both of these people who work harder and fight for a morally good world will receive the least justice in this world and will probably die earlier than their counterparts.

No two people will agree on what's a just world and what's not, even though they might eventually agree on some principles, but they will never agree on what constitutes justice on every issue. As long as you set the meaning of justice, you would make sure that it matches your beliefs, views, and principles. As long as your definition of justice does not collide with your principles and beliefs, then that's something you can defend and protect. However, at the core of justice is goodness and inclusion for you and others. Yet, all that is not coming from life itself. Rather, it requires you to go and get it or take it for yourself. Don't try to look for a just world but rather try to make the world around you just.

Additionally, in life, you are more likely to blame your blunders and bad circumstances on your life and your own luck. Yet, you should learn never to do that, because you are shackling yourself and preventing it from pushing through the many challenges that you face going through life. Your life is like Amazon, the website where you have a Wishlist and a shopping cart. Your Amazon Wishlist won't buy itself. Similar to your own luck full of wishes, hopes, wants, and needs, the Amazon Wishlist won't come along on its own. So, go ahead and move your own luck to the shopping cart and press the purchase button instead of blaming your blunders and struggles on your own life and luck. Go ahead and challenge your own luck and try to go all-in on your disappointments and blunders. Learn to turn your bad luck into a good one by accepting it internally, and challenging it externally. You cannot control many aspects of your life. Therefore, being prepared with plans and contingencies, you force luck into your life and force it to adhere to one of your plans or contingencies. If things don't go as you wish, or if and when disaster strikes, you will be lucky to have been prepared. If things go well and disaster never shows its ugly face, then you can also consider yourself lucky to have things go your way without a struggle.

There are a lot of people with many different definitions and beliefs about what constitutes a just world. Most people will associate the existence of a just world with the existence of a higher power, a God, or some other type of divine justice. Hence, when their views of a just world do not translate into real life and never come to fruition, some of them consequently would deny the existence of a just world, a god, or divine justice. This view of a just world means that morally good people, including men, women, and children, should not face all the cruelty and evil that exists. Therefore, if you take time to contemplate the existence of a just world, a god, or divine justice, you will have to think about all the evil in our world. You will recognize that the evil in this world exists in two forms, either the moral evils which human beings inflict upon each other or the natural evils that seem to strike even the best people. It's normal that the suffering in this world would give you a good reason to reject the existence of a just world, a god, or even divine justice. For if this world was a just one, then innocent people wouldn't die from wars, diseases, earthquakes, tsunamis, and other tragedies that so many innocent people face.

Seeing and going through all the suffering or hardship in your life or others can test yours or others faith in the existence of a fair and just world, a god, and divine justice. However, just because you don't see something with your own eyes does not mean it does not exist. Finding and believing in a fair and just world, the existence of a god, and divine justice will begin with your heart and not only with your head. You will need to satisfy two requirements to fully recognize and see a fair and just world, a god, and divine justice. You will need to have a better understanding of life's fairness and justice, and you will need to modify your twisted and corrupt understanding of what constitutes a fair and just world. By using a combination of your head and heart and by utilizing your logic and beliefs, you will be able to unshackle yourself from your prior misguided beliefs about fairness and justice. Then and only then, you might be able to unlock your full potential and abilities because you will finally understand that life's justice is not about what life gives or takes from you. Rather, it's about what you get and take for yourself.

Finally, the idea of ultimate and complete fairness is one of the few decent and noble things in this life that is worth standing up and fighting for. Aspire to a world of ultimate fairness. Push, fight, and stand up for a just world. When examining your world, you will find out that ultimate fairness and justice are two of the few elements in it that will propel you toward becoming a decent human being. It will help you shape your life to be an exemplary one full of self-righteousness and heavenly gratification and fulfillment. In a fair world, there are no differences between anyone, regardless of their gender, ethnicity, color, and beliefs. Everyone in that fair world is required to contribute and receive equally. Therefore, you should aspire to see a fair world because doing that is your starting point. Practicing justice and committing yourself to being just is your blueprint toward a manifestation of that aspiration. Lastly, don't try to change the world at once. Rather, plan to change it incrementally, because the world is too large and vast for you to change it all at once and alone. Start with yourself and change yourself for the better. The act of working and improving yourself will give you the power to change your surroundings and your community. Eventually, you will be able to change enough people, and that change will hopefully snowball into an unstoppable avalanche of positive change inspired by your own change.

Some tips to help you in correcting and getting a better understanding of fairness and justice, alongside some methods you can utilize to see a fair and just world materialize:

- Aspire to a fair world. Push and work for a just one, because standing up and fighting for justice is your blueprint toward seeing a fair world materialize.

- Understand that life's justice is not about what life gives you or takes from you. Rather, it's about what you get and take for yourself.

- Learn to accept your luck internally. Challenge it and face your fears externally.

- Simplify your outlook on life's fairness and justice. Don't shackle yourself with illusion-filled hopes and wishes for you to be able to push forward with any of the challenges that you might come across in life.

- Always remember that in life, justice and ultimate fairness are two of the few principles that will propel you toward being decent and having a decent life. Don't just be a living being but also try to be a living human being.

CHAPTER TEN

Doing Good, Bad, Or Both

"

You are born with good and bad within you and surrounding you. You grow old with good and bad, and you die with good and bad. Your good can be bad for me, and my good can be bad for you. It all depends on the situation and the circumstances.

In life, good exists because bad exists, similar to light and darkness, life and death, and happiness or sadness. One cannot exist without the other. You cannot tell what is known as good according to your society until you understand and grasp what is known as bad, and vice versa. Each society has its norms, rules, good and bad. Therefore, the meaning of good and bad will vary depending on the society you live in or the society you come from. Still, a lot of societies, cultures, and religions tend to agree on the core meaning and definition of good and bad. Consequently, if you take a broad definition of good and bad, you can state that good means an action by which an entity is morally right and righteous according to that society. On the other hand, bad means an action by which an entity is immoral and wicked according to that society.

Additionally, when discussing the origin of good and bad, taking into consideration the numerous views and beliefs that exist in the world religious or not, they all tend to associate those to a higher entity or a supernatural force. However, by using those same basic, earthly, and known definitions of good and bad and associating them to a higher entity also referred to in many societies/religions as God, some will argue that God is both good and bad. Yet, using those limited definitions, which vary from one society to another, and applying them to a higher superior entity such as God, does not give that higher entity or God justice, and you are not being good to that higher entity or God. The whole idea behind a God or a supernatural power is in its otherworldly superiority above any basic and earthly meaning and understanding. Therefore, for you to be able to judge a higher entity's goodness, you need a higher and more progressive definition of good to match the entity's goodness of which you are trying to judge.

You can do good, bad, or both because the decisions you make not only affect you but also affect the world you inhabit. An action you take on one side of the country can affect another person living on the other side of the country or even the world. That's just a simplistic view of it, which states that every action has a reaction or reactions that trickle down. As you go through life, you will see many examples where people's decisions and actions have an enormous effect on other people's lives. Those effects can be good, bad, or both. An action you think is bad from your point of view can be good and out of love from another's. You can see this with humans as well as animals. For example, you try to pet new born kitten and get scratched or bitten by their mother. Because you were trying to pet the kitten out of love for them, you would think getting bit or scratched is bad, and yet, the mother's reaction of biting you was out of love and protection for her children. You can also be the owner of a company and decide that for your company to keep on growing, you need to fire one of your employees and hire someone else to replace him or her. Within a short period, you hear that the person you fired has died after their life had crumpled since being fired from your company. Does this make your action of firing them bad, and does it also make you a bad person? You can see that in this instance, you ended up doing both good and bad. You did good by your company and made sure to keep it growing and possibly employing and helping even more people. You also hired a new employee and helped in changing their life for the better, hopefully by giving them work and a source of income to provide for themselves and their families. On the other hand, you more likely did a bad action from the point view of the employee that got fired, in which you possibly deprived them of the only income source they had to rely on to keep on living and providing for themselves and their families. The above example illustrates how there is no ultimate evil, and there is no ultimate good. Therefore, when you hear the saying, "always try to find the good in people or occasions," don't just assume that it's just a saying that does not hold any meaning or any truth. Understand that everyone and every action in this world have good and bad within them. On the other hand, it's also understandable that you find it hard to see and look for the good in some of the evil people you meet or in some evil events you see throughout your life. Still, you have the power of using logic, reason, and compassion to differentiate between the good and bad in people and their actions.

There is a reason and wisdom behind the existence of everything in this life. You might take the existence of some things in this life and perceive them as evil and unjust from your point of view, while at the same time, others can perceive them as being good and just. This conflict of interest and belief is just one small and integral part that goes into building out your life and the community you live in. You will need many different elements when trying to build a house, elements such as wood, bricks, sand, and water. Similarly, you will need many different elements when you are building and molding a community. Elements such as men, women, young, old, good and evil. You can use wood, bricks, sand, and water to build a house or a bridge, and you can use the same elements to build a prison or a wall. It all depends on how you use these elements. The same applies when it comes to building a community. Integrating all the elements that exist within a community is so vital for the success of that community. How you use, guide, and integrate those elements "men, woman, young, old, good and evil" together, can either destroy a community and fill it with hate and greed. Alternatively, it can build a strong community that values life, love, justice, and fairness.

Battles between evil and good have been well documented throughout world history, be it in its real history, mythical tales, or other forms of art. Who wins the battle between evil and good was the main theme in all those stories and history. However, eventually, life propels you into realizing that evil will always win more battles than good, and yet good will always win the war. Legacies are the only things that come from these wars between good and evil. Looking through history, you will see that time is not a friend of evil people or evil actions. Time passes, and so do those evil people and evil actions. So far, no evil person has lived forever, but so many good people and good actions are still living through their good legacies to this day.

A lot of religions teach that God is always good and that God gave you free will and the ability to make judgments and choices. They also teach that the cause of suffering and pain is not God. Rather, it's the people's choices and actions. Furthermore, they teach that God gave you a mind and soul, engraved you with compassion to brighten your life, and made you question, research, and study, then evolve and make decisions. Yet, you, as well as many others throughout your lives and struggles, will deny the existence of God for reasons you believe to be true. It is understandable for you and for others to walk away or deny the existence of God because of some bad circumstances or great suffering in your lives. However, as you saw in earlier examples, many circumstances and great suffering you and others face in life do not make God bad or evil. It just illustrates that your or other's choices and judgment can lead to good, bad, or both. Therefore, you can deduce that God is not bad, and neither are you. Your ability to choose and make decisions is something good, while the act of choosing and picking can lead you to something good, bad, or both.

Lastly, understand that you get from the world what you put into it. So, teach yourself always to put good into the world no matter how big or small the act is. Start by showing love for people around you and for people you meet throughout your daily life. Love and respect not only the people in your life, but also other living beings, including animals, trees, and oceans. Additionally, communicate properly to show the goodness in you and to bring the goodness out of people around you. Therefore, you need to learn how to communicate properly in life and with life. You do that by being compassionate and by being empathetic to the people around you, and by understanding and realizing your life purpose and goals, which in turn will help you find the good in each situation that life throws at you.

Most of all, make sure to smile at the people with a frown in their faces the same way you would smile for smiling people. Certainly, smiling at them is different than laughing at them. If you want to be a dumbass, you can go ahead and laugh at them, and you will eventually get what's coming to you: a punch in the face, hopefully. Smiling is the least you can do as a good deed and one of the smallest and least intrusive acts that you can put out into the world. Smiling is the smallest act you can do, and yet it's one of the most powerful gestures you can utilize to break all types of barriers between you and others. It's the only action that does not require any linguistic or cultural translation, as it's universally recognized and understood. Commit yourself and aspire to find the good in people. Instead of killing them with kindness, you should instead aspire to revive them with kindness and give them life, or better yet, energize and help them to bring and shine their life out.

Tips for bringing out the good in people and seeing the good in every situation:

- Recognize that there is no ultimate good or ultimate bad, because in a lot of situations, what's good for you can be bad for others, and what's good for others can be bad for you.

- You can never guarantee that your action will ultimately be good for everyone involved and affected. Still, you can reach a close enough result by bringing out the good in you, and by utilizing your logic, heart, empathy, and compassion.

- Understand that you will receive from the world what you put into it, and it can be both materialistic or non-materialistic things that you will receive. You just need to recognize and appreciate it.

- Learn to communicate properly in life and with life. Communication is important to show the goodness in you and to bring the goodness out of people around you.

- Remember always to show your smile because it's the least intrusive good act you can do with the most power. It will help you break all and any barrier you might face with people and with life itself, so go ahead and show your beautiful smile.

CHAPTER ELEVEN

Utilizing free will and embracing destiny

> **"**
>
> You can make choices and decisions, but you can't choose
> the consequences or control the result.

Do you have a free will to choose and do what you like? Or is it just destiny in disguise, and all you do is just act upon it?

Free will is a debatable subject for lots of people, and it has been for many decades. People grappled with the idea of free will because, throughout their lives, they struggle to control some if not most of the situations they are put in and face daily. So, on the one hand, they know they don't have complete free will, nor do they have complete control over their lives or actions. On the other hand, they still choose to believe in the existence of free will and in their power to rule over their lives and choices. They do so because that belief allows them to live in a civilized, just, and fair world, where people are responsible for their actions and can enjoy all the good results from those actions. They can also face any repercussions from those same actions. Hence, believing in the existence of free will in its core stems from self-motivated and self-serving principles, which grow bigger and bigger as people keep evolving, exploring, and integrating.

When you are just a baby, you have not yet reached a mental state in which you can comprehend and realize your power of choosing and decision-making. You rely on your parents and caretakers to make decisions and choices for you, be it things you eat, the time you sleep, things you wear, and activities you do. As soon as you reach an age where you realize your power of free will, you become a monster literally. Your self-serving motives start ruling over your decision-making at a young age, and it molds and shapes your outlook on life and the people within it. Your belief in your own free will develops and becomes stronger as you grow older, both mentally and physically, through the time as a baby, teen, to an adult.

Now, other living beings such as animals in all their types and breeds can still have some form of free will as well. They can utilize it to choose their favorite food out of all that you provide for them. They can choose to jump in the water or sleep, and they can feel guilty, sad, or happy. With animals' abilities to choose or feel, still, their mental capacities and free will are miniature when compared to those of humans. Human free will is exponentially greater than that of animals. Not only for their ability to recognize collective consequences and feel collective guilt but, most importantly, for their ability to comprehend their own foresight capacity. Their foresight capacity which allows them to anticipate and predict the outcomes of their actions. Despite all that, figuring out whether humans have free will or not is not as important as actually believing and adhering to its core meaning. Therefore, when assuming the most simplistic definition of free will, which is the power of acting without the constraint of fate and destiny, you can deduce that you, as a human being, do have some type of free will and freedom. However, based on the many events that happen throughout your life, you can also deduce that you don't have complete and ultimate freedom. You can think you have control over your life. Still, the majority of what happens in your life is out of your control, and your free will reach. You don't have complete free will, not even over your own body.

For example, I can tell you the sky is green, and the ocean is black, and just by doing that and as long as you can understand the words I am saying and the languages I am speaking, you will inadvertently picture a green sky and black ocean. Hence, you can see that you don't have complete free will, not even when it comes to your own imagination or even your dreams. Yet, if you didn't have free will to make choices and decisions in life at all, then you can say that everything you do in this life, whether good or bad, is not because of your choices as a human being. Rather, it's because of the superior power ruling over you and controlling every move and decision that you make.

Let us say that you, alongside everyone else, started using your lack of free will as the excuse for your actions, then that will lead to the eventual collapse of every community in this world. By freeing yourself from responsibility and by blaming everything but yourself for your actions, especially when it comes to those actions that are immoral or bad with severe consequences and repercussions, then you are shaking up the principles that each community is built on. The lack of belief in the existence of free will itself will deprive each community of its justice system. It will strip each community of its good morals, and it will destroy every civilization. For if there is no free will, then no one can be held accountable for their misdeeds. If there are no consequences for terrible misdeeds, then both principles of fairness and justice will deteriorate, and civilization will cease to exist.

Certainly, that's not the case here because you, as a human being, have partial free will as well as the ability to make choices and judgments every day of your life. You have the power of free will combined with the ability of decision-making to take ownership of your life and your own decisions. Free will and the ability to make decisions empower you to do good, bad, or both. It empowers you to build or destroy, search and research, love or hate, teach or learn, and pick and choose. You, as a human being, are responsible for your own decisions and actions because that action and decision cannot happen without your consent to do so.

There is a lot of evidence that confirms the existence of your free will, one of which is your ability to self-correct. You can pick and choose, and you can make good and bad decisions in your daily life, and then you can choose to celebrate those good decisions while choosing to learn and correct the bad decisions. The only way you can disregard and dismiss your own free will is when you decide not to utilize your self-correcting ability and when you choose to forgo learning and searching and researching for more knowledge from books and from life itself. Your self-correcting ability is important when it comes to proving the existence of your own free will because it illustrates how you can choose to correct a mistake you made. It empowers you to learn from experiences throughout your life. You start utilizing your self-correcting ability from a young age, and you decide to learn from all the experiences you go through, such as the first time eating hot food and getting burned. You learn and decide to cool off your food before eating it. When you first get burned touching a stove, you decide and learn that moving forward; you will be more cautious dealing with hot objects. When you see an immoral action, you decide to stand up against it and fix it. These are all lessons and experiences you go through in life. You choose and decide to learn from and to grow and mature and to be a better you, all of which won't materialize without utilizing your own free will.

You go through life thinking that you have a lot of control over your own life, but in reality, there are so many outside influences that factor in when it comes to your actions and decision-making. Examples of such factors include but are not limited to social norms and societal pressures, religious teachings, guardians' gaudiness, instincts, fear, and drugs. All the ones listed and many others not listed can contribute to your actions or decision-making. Your background, your mental and physical constitution, your upbringing, who brought you up, and the morals and beliefs engraved in your psyche are all factors that affect the way you act and the method in which you make decisions. Most importantly, you as a human being control less in your own life than what you believe, especially when it comes to life and death, two major events that happen for every human. You, alongside others, share these two common major events that you have no control over, no matter what actions, paths, or choices you make in life. You have no control over being born or not; neither do you have any control over your own death.

All human beings have free will and freedom to choose their actions and reactions in life. It's free will when your decision is made without any influence from an outside source, and you are exercising your freedom when you know every decision you make is your own. Free will and destiny are closely related in that you can choose and decide on doing something, but while in the act, it can easily within seconds turn to be ruled by destiny. You started the act exercising your free will and end up following your destiny. Likewise, you can also face a situation in which you had no control whatsoever, but while going through that situation, you can utilize your free will and take control. In other words, free will and destiny are so intertwined that the existence of free will does not mean the non-existence of destiny because free will and destiny can work together in every action and reaction that you make in your life.

You chose to read this book, you picked up the book, and opened this page and started reading. You can choose to continue reading this chapter, or you can choose to skip it and continue reading other sections, or you can put the book down and stop reading. By choosing to read or not to read the book, you can say that you exercised your free will. On the other hand, you can also be influenced by an outside source, such as losing power and losing all the means that would allow you to continue reading the book. You can also get an emergency call from family or friends that forces you to put down the book and leave. You decided to put down the book, but this was not done according to your free will, but rather it was done according to the ongoing life processes in your destiny.

Each of the decisions you make will lead to a different path and a different ending or another beginning. Life has so many endings and so many beginnings. You, as a human being in this life, have so many different endings and beginnings depending on your own choices and decisions in your daily life. Understand that you can always change your destiny and believe in the power you have, which you can utilize to change and mold your destiny. With all the different paths you can choose to follow; still, you can end up with the same result and the same ending no matter what path you choose. On the other hand, by trying different routes and never shying away from challenges, you can also reach a different ending, keeping in mind that a different ending here does not mean an ending where nothing will come or exist after. Rather, it can mean an end to a beginning or a beginning to an end.

In life, you must choose the group of people you want to be associated with, the lucky ones, or the not so lucky ones. Once you choose this group, and as long as you keep persisting, the breaks in life that count are coming, and they will eventually materialize. When you choose to be in the lucky ones' group, you, in turn, decide to go through life tolerating everything that life throws at you, the good or the bad. You learn to accept your luck, and you become at peace with it internally, while repelling and fighting it externally. It does not matter whether you believe in the cause and effect principle, or a divine power with good and bad deeds, or in reciprocal karma. Even though they might differ in some of their teachings, still, at their core, they all teach that once you provide the cause, you will eventually feel the effect. You perform a morally good act, and you receive a good reward and vice versa. You perform an immoral act, and you receive punishment and reciprocal karma and a bad result. Life is like a barista, in which you go into a coffee shop. Sometimes you will get a free drink or a cookie just by being there at the right place at the right time. However, most of the time, the barista will wait for you to order your coffee and pay for it, and only then will you receive that tasty coffee you ordered and paid for.

Likewise, sometimes life will throw at you some free goods and happiness, but most of the time, you will have to look and work for your cup of joy, happiness, and luck. You will have to pay for all of that with hard work, patience, praying, and persistence.

Alongside free will and the ability to make judgments and choices, you, as a human being, also have some unquantifiable assets such as your mind, compassion, and ability for self-correction. These are just some tools and instruments that enhance your free will. Having a mind, compassion, and combined with the ability for self-correcting have always been some of the most important pillars when trying to utilize your free will, especially when combined with your judgment and decision-making powers. These assets are all variables that change as long as you keep on evolving, learning, searching, and researching. Therefore, as you mature and grow mentally and physically, you will eventually notice that your views, emotions, desires, decisions, and actions change along the way. Having free will and being able to make decisions and perform actions is what makes your life meaningful. It's what makes you wake up every day looking forward to the future because you know that you have something that gives you hope for a better, easier, healthier, full of love, and brighter tomorrow. Hence, you, as a human, have free will and other unquantifiable assets such as a mind, compassion, and self-correcting ability, all of which are morally good at their core. Yet, the way you use free will alongside the other assets you have, whether good or bad or both, is all up to you.

Lastly, you, cannot control or rule over a lot of different aspects of your life, such as life, death, dreams, and imagination. Still, you do have limited free will and freedom to choose and make decisions. It's also important for you and others to believe in the existence of your own free will because believing in its existence is one of the few elements in your life that will keep you from surrendering to an unlucky and hopeless life. Believing in the existence of free will for you and others will help in sustaining justice for each community. It will help to improve civilization because everyone will be held responsible for their actions, good or bad. Your free will and freedom of making decisions are limited. Yet, by putting your free will to work, and by exercising your freedom, you are unlocking all the secrets and riddles hidden within you. You are bringing about your own luck and your truth. So, use your free will with caution and exercise your freedom with mindfulness and compassion.

Things to always remember when going through life, maturing, learning about yourself, your life, free will, and destiny:

- Your free will is a product of your maturation and growth. The more you grow and learn, gain knowledge in life, and about life, the more you are able to embrace your free will, and the stronger you will believe in its existence.

- Your destiny and your own free will are closely tied together, so learn to treat your fate and destiny with acceptance internally, and challenge anything and everything externally. Just know that you always have the choice to change your circumstances or choose to accept or not accept those circumstances.

- You should always try to utilize your logic, compassion, and self-correcting ability alongside of your own free will. Choose and decide on the best outlook and the optimum foreseeable future not only for you but also for your family, community, and the world around you.

- Embracing your free will and believing in its existence will help you live in a just world. It will push you to seek a more just world and a better, happier life for you and others. So, make sure to treat your time with eagerness and patience, regardless of all its obstacles and turbulent events. Treat your family with softness and your brothers/sisters with forgiveness.

- There are many ways to get to where you want in life. You just need to decide and choose to get to it.

CHAPTER TWELVE

Being in tune with your mind & soul

"

There is a soul and a spirit, and then there is a mind that
acts as a vessel and fuses the two.

Do you have a spirit, a soul, and a mind? And what is the relationship between your spirit and your body?

Your soul is the start of all beginnings for you as a human being. It's the source that gives your body and mind the energy they need to function and perform each task in your daily life. On the other hand, your spirit is the combination of your emotions, persona, and your own self. It's what holds your emotions and feelings. It's the entity that gets angry and sad. In life, you can always mold and build a spirit, and you can also fix a broken spirit. Whereas, your body is a mere vessel for your soul. Without a soul, there is no life for you as a person and a living being in this world. Your soul comes first to revive and insert energy and life into your body. Then your body comes alive and can move and function, utilizing the energy coming from that soul. Then your spirit grows with you as you grow, and you eventually learn how to build it and learn all that affects it. You become acquainted with what affects it positively or negatively, and that which lifts it up or brings it down.

There is a soul and a spirit, and then there is a mind that acts as a vessel and fuses the two. It's the same case for all living beings when they all begin their circle of life with a soul and a body. Yet, science has proven the existence of a brain and a complex nervous system in humans. Additionally, a lot of scientific studies have stated that the complex nervous system in humans is the one thing that makes them different and superior to other living organisms. Moreover, in conjunction with these scientific facts, there exists some other ideologies and beliefs and what science calls theories and hypotheses. These theories and hypotheses state that the main difference and assets which allow humans to be superior to other living organism is the existence of a nonphysical mind and a spirit alongside their complex nervous system.

Science refers to these as theories and hypotheses for many reasons. One justification for doubting the existence of a nonphysical mind, a soul, and a spirit, is the lack of accessibility to examine these entities the way you can study and examine a physical one. Some of these theories which support the existence of a nonphysical mind and a spirit cannot be proven using the same methods and processes used scientifically. However, you cannot discredit those nonphysical hypotheses just because you cannot prove their accuracy using the same scientific processes and methods. Therefore, even though they cannot be proven using the same scientific methods, that does not take away from the fact that they provide so many valid arguments that even science cannot ignore. An example of such arguments is how the mind and the brain are not one entity. Although the brain controls a lot of your activities and emotions, yet, the mind has a power independent of the brain's activities. For instance, nobody can tell you what you are thinking by measuring your brain waves. You must be asked about what you are thinking. Additionally, science has proven that consciousness continues even after a person's brain has stopped functioning, and he or she has been declared dead. Hence, there are many medical cases where people wake up from a long coma or after being declared dead and report being aware of things happening around them.

Lastly, the body and the mind are not identical. For if they were identical, then everything true for one is also true for the other. The mind and the body, including the brain, are two separate entities. If we change something about the body, that does not mean we change the same thing about the mind as well. Still, both the body and mind work together in forming human beings, and what links the mind and body is the entity called the brain. The mind appears united and unified with the whole body. However, when an arm or any other part of the body is cut off, the mind is not aware of any removal made to the body. Therefore, you will hear a lot of people who lost part of their body but still felt pain in those body parts that they lack. Hence, even though it's a fact that those people lack some part of their body, this is only true for the physical body and not the mind. It's not true for the mind because the mind is not aware of any absent part from the body. It's still functioning as if those missing parts were still attached. Thus, you can deduce that the mind is not identical to the body and that both the mind and the body are distinct entities.

Each living being has a distinct spirit and a distinct soul, and yet, humans differ from other living beings in one important aspect in that they have a more advanced consciousness and a more self-aware spirit. There are certain amounts of external elements and a certain energy required for you to receive the assistance you need to unlock the knowledge of your nonphysical mind and spirit. You will not benefit from having a mirror without having the required light for that mirror to reflect your image. Your spirit here is the mirror, and all other external elements and the energy required are the light that will allow your spirit to reflect its truth. Those required external elements such as faith, intuition, science, or all combined, are all variables and depend largely on you as a person. You will need some or all of those elements to exist in your life. Their existence will help you go through all the conflicts and disagreements you experience in your life. Once enough of these elements appear within you and your life, you will gain knowledge that allows your nonphysical and physical entities to co-exist. It will give your nonphysical entities the energy it needs to shine through you. Then and only then you will able to see, acknowledge, and understand yourself, and you will be able to realize the existence of your nonphysical entities.

The mind is a nonphysical entity that is distinct from the body and can exist without it. The mind is not an extended thing and nothing but a thinking element, whereas the body, is an extended and non-thinking thing. The mind has power for special modes of consciousness and other sensations such as love, hate, doubt, and understanding. However, it's not logically acceptable to associate these characteristics to extended, non-thinking things like stones and rocks. In contrast, it is not logically acceptable to associate characteristics of quantity, shape, and size to non-extended and thinking things. The only way for you as humans to realize that you exist is for your mind to exist before your body does. You can be certain that you exist because you are a thinking being and not because you can feel your body. In other words, your body is not perceived by your senses or other faculties of the imagination but by the intellect alone. This perception of your body is derived not from being touched or seen but from being understood.

When looking scientifically at proving the existence of a spirit, a soul, and a nonphysical mind, you will struggle to do so using the same ordinary method you usually use to study actual physical things. Your mind is more than just your brain and has a non-material, spiritual dimension that includes consciousness and possibly an eternal attribute. Science can prove the existence of physical things, like a brain and a complex nervous system that governs and controls an abundance of human abilities and actions. However, it does not mean it is accurate to assume the non-existence of other nonphysical things such as a mind, a spirit, and a soul. In other words, proving the existence of one does not mean proving the non-existence of another. It just means that using the same methods and the same processes for proving one thing cannot be used universally to prove something else. The brain and the body are physical entities, and the reason why human knowledge of them is growing so much faster because it's possible to perform all kinds of experiments on them directly. Whereas, the mind, spirit, and soul are nonphysical entities. Human knowledge of them is incomparable to their knowledge of the brain and the body because it's harder to study and experiment on those nonphysical entities, especially when using the same methods for studying physical entities.

If your spirit is a car, then your soul would be the power source or the gasoline that makes it run. Your car can break down, and you can still fix it and drive it again, but when your car is out of its energy source and gasoline, you can no longer drive it even if there is nothing broken down or wrong with it. Whether you are a believer in the existence of the afterlife or not, you should always think of your soul as a very expensive loaner, which you will be able to use for some time, be it a day, a week, or even years. After that time ends, it will be reclaimed, and you will be forced to return it. By understanding that it's a loaner and that you will be charged extra fees for any damages to it, you, in turn, will make sure to cradle and take better care of it. Once you acknowledge that it's up to you whether you return your soul in a good, decent, or bad condition, you will push yourself to take better care of it. You will utilize it properly, which, consequently, will guarantee you a more satisfying life and a more fulfilling existence.

Some tips and suggestions for realizing your existence and for working with and molding your spirit:

- Think of your soul as a very expensive loaner. You don't own it, but you are solely responsible for its health and wellbeing. Thinking of it this way will push you to cradle it and take better care of it.

- Work on building your spirit by practicing self-love and positive affirmation, by finding love in your life, and giving it back to the world around.

- Always be true to yourself and always push yourself toward things that provide you with satisfaction and fill your world with joy.

- Practice meditation and praying to avoid being negative in your life, and always let go of your negative feelings and emotions.

- Make sure to always live in the moment and at present. Avoid living in your past or holding on to it.

Chapter THIRTEEN

Unlocking the beauty of life

"

The beauty of life is easy to spot, see, and feel, and the only

way you can block yourself from seeing it and feeling it is

by closing your eyes, mind, and heart.

Be open to living life with all its challenges, issues, and experiences. Don't treat it as a problem to be solved but rather as a reality to be lived and experienced. The beauty and joy of life lies in its questions, doubts, and uncertainty. For you to enjoy life, you will need these doubts and questions that challenge and contradict your beliefs, ideologies, and convictions. The internal conflicts that happen inside you will eventually lead you to enjoy life in the symbolic sense of the word. Those questions and doubts act as nourishment for your brain and soul. The more questions you have, the more answers you will try to find by pushing yourself through and into new experiences. The act of trying to find answers to these questions and the process and the journey you go through trying to find these answers is at the heart of life's beauty and one of the main sources of finding joy in this life. Sometimes you will find joy in finding answers to these questions, and other times, the joy will be in not finding any answers at all. A life without questions and doubts which challenge your beliefs and convictions is a life without joy.

One of the main reasons why you can go in life without finding real joy is because you become another casualty of life's gravity. You get sucked into trying to navigate around and between the obstacles and challenges that life throws at you. That's one of the biggest mistakes that you can make, to think of these challenges and issues as a problem that you must solve to be able to enjoy life. Again, you must realize that life is not a problem to be solved but a reality to be experienced and enjoyed. These obstacles and challenges are part of what makes life interesting and fun. All the situations, challenges, and experiences you go through will only bring about joy and contentment, especially if you keep resisting life's gravity, and as long as you keep working on the inquisitive kid within you. In other words, once you can face and go through each and every challenge, as long as you can keep your desire for learning and asking questions alive and burning, then and only then will you be able to find joy in every situation in life.

You should try living life as it's supposed to be lived, with logic and simplicity in all its aspects. Yet, you should never take anything at face value or believe in something just because your parents, family, friends, community, and others believe it. You should never believe in someone else's truth. Rather, you should always try finding your own truth by questioning everything around you, starting with creation, evolution, and ending with your existence and any higher power existence. If you search and research using all the brainpower, intuition, and desires you have, you will eventually find a truth that satisfies your beliefs and intuition. Open your eyes to see the beauty of life and open your mind to all the questions and uncertainty that life presents to you. Doing so with an open heart to love and to be loved, as long as you keep searching, researching, and evolving, you will always find a truth that satisfies you and consequently realize and grasp all that makes life beautiful and joyful.

You are equipped with physical and psychological abilities and mental capacities since the day you were born. These various abilities which exist in every human being start at a novice stage and develop as time passes and as that person develops, learns, and goes through all the different life experiences. Using these various abilities and all the lessons you learn from these different experiences, you will be able to form and mold your life and make it as happy or sad, joyful or miserable as you would want it to be. Do not allow your experiences to define you or to mold your life. Rather, make sure that you define you, and you mold your own life the way you see fit. You're probably wondering and asking yourself how you can switch the script of a failed experience to be a successful one. The answer is as simple as you just do. In life, you go through an experience. It may be considered a failure according to societal norms, but you do not have to accept social norms. You can decide to see your experience as a successful one. At the end of the day, once you are confident in living your life your way and you have paid your dues, no one has the right to tell you otherwise. Your experiences are yours only, and the only time your experience would be a real failure is if you never learn anything from it. So, make sure to learn from them, the bad before the good, and use what you learned to mold your own life and future.

You, alongside all other human beings, already have the two most important instruments that will help you in bringing about and producing joy in your life. You don't need to buy these instruments, and you don't have to learn them either because they already exist within you. You just need to utilize them. Those two instruments that hold all that power are curiosity and imagination. You need to be curious and inquisitive like a kid. You need to imagine the world your own way. Avoid imagining or thinking of the world just like everyone else does, because you are not them and they are not you. You are your own being with different likes, wants, and needs. Therefore, going along thinking of the world just like everyone else does or as an out-of-the-box thinker might not work for you. However, what will work for you is forming your own shape and being your own thinker. For, in curiosity and imagination, you will find the answer to your happiness and joy. The only way for you to move forward in life and to find your happiness is to be curious and open to new challenges and new experiences and to embrace and welcome your fear of new experiences and challenges. Your fear is one of the main factors that is blocking you from discovering the beauty of life and happiness. Your fear of new experiences, challenges, failure, and success, and your fear of the unknown are all deciding factors of whether you discover the beauty of life or not. By allowing your fear to take over your decision-making and allowing it to control every move you make in your life, you rob yourself of the experiences you need to find real joy in life. You don't realize that at the end of fear is the most joy that you could possibly get or achieve. So, confront your fears.

Life is simple, and it is meant to be lived as such. You, as well as others, add a lot of seriousness and pressure into it and on yourself. The pressure of acting a certain way, sticking to social norms, and going by what's acceptable versus what is simple, correct, and logical. Start thinking of life as a kid again, because whatever issue or challenge you are facing will eventually pass, no matter what the challenge or the issue is and regardless of whether you stress about it or not. You might think it's hard to do such a thing, but let me give you a simple example to show how easy this concept is to implement.

The upcoming month's rent is due in one week, and you have no means to pay it off. So, you stress about it for a whole week, and at the end of the month, you still couldn't come up with the rent. You worked your hardest and stressed about it for some time, and you still came up empty with no rent, no shelter, and got a few other stress-related illnesses. Similarly, you could've worked hard, and instead of stressing yourself out, you decided to pack your things and be prepared for the result of being homeless. At the end of the issue or challenge, you are facing is just another sharp turn in your life. That sharp turn can be good or bad. You just need to adjust, recalibrate, and tackle the issue from a different angle without being stuck to what's socially acceptable and what's normal. Like the saying, "when life gives you lemons, make some lemonade." If you don't like lemonade, don't stress about it, and just drink the water without any lemons, because at the end of the day, it's your life and it's all about what you want and desire to do with it.

Your life is a never-ending book full of chapters, heroes, and villains. You will always lose some battles to the villains, and sometimes you will have to forfeit some other battles. If your fighting spirit is alive and well, as long as you stay open to new challenges, you will always win the war, especially if you make sure to learn from all that you go through, the good and the bad. Life is beautiful with its struggles and sad moments, or happy and joyous moments. Thus, you should try to enjoy every moment in your life, because as time and years go by, you will be looking back at those years and experiences you hated or resented so much. It will strike you that your years of struggle were the most beautiful years of your life because those years made you the person you are today. As life and years move forward, you tend to forget that between your challenging life and struggles, you had some happy moments. After those happy moments, you faced some struggles again, then happy moments, and so on. Life is like a roller coaster with ups and downs, filled with excitements and disappointments. So, enjoy the excitements and live through its disappointments to arrive at its happiness.

Tips for experiencing joy and bring about all the joy that life can offer you:

- Open your eyes to see the beauty of life. Open your mind to all the questions and uncertainty that life presents to you.

- Open your heart to love and to be loved. As long as you keep searching, researching, and evolving, you will always find a truth that satisfies you. Consequently, you will realize and grasp all that makes life beautiful and joyful.

- Resist life's gravity. Don't allow the issues and challenges you face in your life to drag you into the black hole of life where you are only able to see and feel resentment and dislike for your life and everything around it and in it.

- Keep working on the inquisitive kid within you. Keep your desire for learning and asking questions alive and burning, because it will push you toward bringing joy into your life.

- Live your life the way you see fit, without the added pressure of acting a certain way, sticking to the social norms or going by what's acceptable versus what is simple, correct, and logical.

- Start thinking of life as a kid again, because your issue or challenge will eventually pass, no matter it is and regardless of whether you stress about it or not.

- Remind yourself always to live life in the present and not in the past nor the future. Nothing in this world has more joy for you than the present time.

- Push yourself to go through new experiences and never let fear dictate what you should or should not do, because at the end of fear is the most joy you can experience.

CHAPTER FOURTEEN

Safeguarding your hopes and dreams

> **"**
>
> Your hopes are the pen by which you can write your future.
> Whereas, your faith is the ink filling that pen used to write
> the pages of your life. Picking up the pen and learning how
> to use it for writing the future of your life is the action
> required for your hopes and faith to be fused and utilized
> correctly and accurately.

There are hopes, faith, and actions, and then there is positive thinking, negative thinking, and reality-based thinking.

In life, your positive thinking is equivalent to your hope and optimism and imagination for a better tomorrow and a better future. You cannot live your life without hoping or wishing for something that will energize and push you through life with its ups and downs. Having hopes and optimism in your life allows you to breathe in and breathe out. It gives you a reason to keep on pushing through all the obstacles and issues you face in your life, and it energizes you to wake up every day looking for new challenges. All the hopes and dreams you have are forever changing. They are not a constant in your life and they will change as you grow, mature, and go through different experiences in your life.

You can have so many hopes and dreams for yourself. You can supplement that with all the faith in the world. Still, you can drag yourself into failure trying to achieving those hopes and dreams. You drag yourself into unexpected failure when you become satisfied with all that you have accomplished so far in your life. One thing you to avoid falling into while working toward accomplishing your hopes and dreams is the false sense of accomplishment. It will derail you from trying to accomplish more of your dreams. It will distract you from reaching a greater and higher level within that dream. You should always be content with each accomplishment you achieve as well as every failed attempt. A failed attempt is just another part of the road toward accomplishing your dreams. However, you should avoid being satisfied with those accomplishments or failed attempts, especially if you want to keep on pushing for greatness in all that you do or want to do.

Never put a ceiling on your hopes and dreams, but rather add to them and renew your commitment to them as you grow, mature, and go through your life journey. Having a ceiling for your hopes and dreams and shying away from enhancing and adding to them is the same as having an expiration date for your life. For if and when you can achieve and reach the ceiling of all that you hoped for, you have hit that date stamp for your death, mentally, emotionally, and sometimes even physically. Your life has a direct correlation with your hopefulness, and without your hopes and dreams to fill your sphere, you will be a mere empty, lifeless vessel. Therefore, be greedy in your hopefulness and teach yourself how to differentiate between being satisfied or just being simply too lazy to achieve more. Remember that in life, you need to be ambitious in order to be greedy, but you don't have to be greedy in order for you to be ambitious.

Additionally, your reality-based thinking is equivalent to your actions and has a strong effect on your future outlook, and your success, or failure. Therefore, in life, make sure to commit yourself to perform all the necessary actions for without performing and accomplishing those actions, your hopes and positive thinking will not materialize. Have a positive outlook toward your life with all its successes and failures, and aspire to do the right thing instead of doing what you like. Learn to listen and understand every piece of advice and criticism, no matter how harsh or blunt it is. Integrating reality-based thinking into your life does not mean admitting your loss before you even start your journey. Rather, it means accepting all the possible outcomes and believing that you can win and win big but that you could also lose. Believing that loss is a possibility that can happen while you are working on your dreams will only push you further toward coming up big and toward succeeding in all that you do. While working toward that which you hope and wish for, there are a lot of essential steps you are required to perform to bring success into your life. Yet, success will never come about without patience. You can hope and wish for something, but without action, acceptance, and patience, you will not attain that which you wish and hope for.

Furthermore, your negative thinking is equivalent to doubt in your faith, your faith in yourself, and your future with all its plans and contingencies. Having a healthy amount of negative thinking in your life is similar to having a healthy amount of doubt in your faith. Having a healthy amount of negative thinking will supercharge your planning abilities and will keep you prepared and ready with a primary plan and a secondary plan. Likewise, having a healthy amount of doubt in your faith, religious or not, will push you toward searching and researching to understand more about yourself and your faith. Going through all these different stages of doubting, searching and researching, will only solidify and strengthen your faith. It will allow you to understand it better. Eventually, you will be more skilled at utilizing it to navigate through all the issues and challenges that life throws at you. Your faith in yourself, in your abilities, and your future take center stage when it comes to all your successes or failures in life. It encourages you to push yourself through new challenges, and it inspires you to dive into new life adventures such as love, business, science, and other similar experiences that require a bit of self-belief and a hint of faith. It teaches you to aspire to and fight for what you dream of even if all the signs and people expect and forecast your eventual failure. Your faith in yourself, your plans and contingencies, and ideas and beliefs are the only thing that will keep you going.

Hopes, actions, and faith are interchangeable and tightly connected. One cannot materialize without another. You act because you hope you will end up with the result that you desire. You hope and wish for something, and you do every action to bring you closer to achieving what you hope for. Then you learn to utilize your faith as the bridge that brings the two together. All three are connected because having faith is believing whatever you imagined and hoped for your future is going to happen eventually and will become a reality no matter the issue or the obstacle you might face. Your faith keeps your hopes alive and keeps you persistent in finishing all the actions necessary to achieve your hopes, dreams, and goals. Therefore, you will need to learn how to maintain, strengthen, and protect your faith, because it's a necessary bridge to keep your hopes alive, pushing you toward finishing and solving all the tasks and issues for you to achieve your dreams. For you to maintain your faith, you will need to surround it with patience and knowledge. For patience is the foundation that solidifies the faith you have, while knowledge is the main pillar that strengthens it. If faith is the bridge between your hopes and actions, then patience is the glue that keeps everything together.

For your hopes to become a reality, you will need to push yourself through all the actions required. Keep in mind that at some point in your life, while you are working on achieving your hopes and dreams, you will face some questions and situations that will plant some doubt in the faith you have in your dreams. Those doubts will visit you in many different forms. One of these forms is the trickiest to spot and originates from within you. This doubt comes about when you achieve a notable milestone on your way to making your dreams a reality. Then, as a result of that achievement, you become lazy for accomplishing more because you fall into a flawed sense of accomplishment. It's a flawed sense because you have convinced yourself that you are satisfied with what you have reached and achieved. You poured water and threw sand on your burning desires and stopped pursuing more of your dream, even though it's obvious that what you have achieved and reached is not at the heights of your hopes and dreams. This specific form of doubt is the trickiest because you are the one chaining yourself to a false sense of limit on your dreams. You are the one doubting your ability to achieve and accomplish more. Thus, be aware of all the pitfalls of your successes and achievements. Stay alert and keep yourself in check to prevent from falling into a false sense of accomplishment that can derail you from achieving more of your dreams. You will need to commit yourself to be hopeful about your future at all times while trying to have more ambition than what your imagination allows. Supplement your hopes and dreams with a proper level of faith in your ability to achieve those dreams and ambitions. Only then will you have enough fuel to push through all the tasks and struggles in your path to reach what you hope for. Be patient, and make sure never to leave a stone unturned while working on achieving what you hope for. Try out all possible methods and techniques available to you and at your disposal. Use your hopes and dreams alongside your faith to write your future until you realize your purpose in life or until your time comes.

Steps to accomplish more of your dreams, keep your hopes alive, and your faith strong:

- Learn to have patience in everything you do in your life.

- Plan your future positively and keep all the negative outcomes and the contingencies of your plans within your sights.

- Make sure always to live your present realistically.

- Learn from all issues and challenges you face in life, but most importantly, keep your eyes on the prize and focus on the final result to keep your hopes alive and your faith strong.

- Stay grounded and never let your success derail you from reaching higher or from achieving more of your dreams and goals. Keep a close watch on yourself and avoid falling into a false sense of accomplishment.

- You, alongside everyone else in this life, will have your time of success. You just need to be looking for it. So, be patient and be looking and working for your time so that you don't miss it when it finally comes around. Your hopes and dreams are only waiting for you to perform the required tasks for them to happen and materialize.

- Accept all the support you can get, and make sure to give all the support you can to those who need it.

- Learn to enjoy and celebrate the process and the journey on the way to achieving those hopes and dreams more than enjoying the result.

PART THREE

Living life and experiencing the world around you

Chapter FIFTEEN

Enjoying life

> **"**
>
> Live your life rather than allowing your life to live through
> you.

A day will come when you realize that you have more past than you have a future. Only then will you be able to learn how to live your life in the moment. You will learn to have a greater appreciation for everything in your life, the smaller things before the big things. Don't wait until time hits you with a hammer on the head for you to decide to slow down your world and enjoy it to the max. Slowing down your world does not equal not finding joy in anything fast or different, such as fast adventures, and newer technology, or a different way of living and different lifestyles. Rather, it means finding all the joy within all of that while avoiding all the bad routines that clog and fill your present time. To do that, you can make two major changes in your life, starting by breaking all the rules and guidelines that contribute to you having a joyless, fast-paced life. Second, learn how to bring nostalgia into your present time while fighting off all that pushes you toward having a life filled with bad routines.

In life, you do things fast, and you want things done fast, not because they taste good nor because they feel good or that you enjoy them. Rather, it's because they taste bad and feel bad, and you just want them to be over. You want the work you do to finish quickly, not because you enjoy it, but because you hate it and would like to be doing something else entirely. You take medicine and try to swallow it before your taste buds can even react to it because you don't like the taste of it. Likewise, fast food is never better than well-prepared, home-cooked food. So, decide to live your life at your pace because you have all that is required to do so. Treat your life like a hot cup of coffee. If you drink it too fast, you burn your tongue and never get a good taste of it, and you are left with a burned tongue. Or you can also treat it like an ice-cold drink. If you chug it fast, you won't enjoy it, and will never get a good taste of it. Hence, you should always strive for a balanced pace that allows you to enjoy your world to the max.

Bringing nostalgia into your present time

One of the best things you can grasp early in life is that you can bring nostalgia into your present time. Nostalgia is a big part of your as well as others' lives because it reminds you of the best things you had or experienced throughout your life. From your favorite food and snacks as a kid, favorite holidays, your time at school with friends, to favorite TV shows or music you used to watch or listen to while growing up. You long for it or wish for some part of it to come back because it reminds you of a simpler time when things were easier for you when you were worry-free or your worries seem miniature in comparison to those in your present time. Those days you are nostalgic about are gone and will not come back no matter how nostalgic you become. They are gone for many reasons but mainly because you, as a person, will mature and grow through the years. They are gone because your priorities, likes, and dislikes will change through the years as well.

Additionally, they are gone because time itself is not a constant, and it will change. It's not going to wait for you, nor is it going to stay unchanged. Therefore, you should try bringing nostalgia into your present time by slowing your time down and enjoying every bit of it. By being appreciative of the things you have, little or not, good and bad, and the journey you are going through regardless of how hard or easy it is. You should try doing that because it's the surefire way you can bring joy into your present time. You should do that because, in a few years, you will be nostalgic about the current time that you are disregarding without appreciation, the same way you are always nostalgic about your past.

Slowing down your world

If you never slow down your world, you are not living your optimum and ultimate life. Nothing in this world that is worth doing is correctly done nor performed well when it's done or performed at a fast pace. You must have heard that what comes fast, goes even faster, and things that take longer to achieve are more rewarding, taste better, and satisfy even more, be it physically, mentally, or emotionally. By not slowing down your world and enjoying every activity or every process you do or finish while going through your life journey, you miss out on gaining some valuable lessons, mental and emotional. Those valuable lessons can only be experienced by slowing the world around you by taking your time going through those activities and journeys. Learn to appreciate and love every activity and experience you do or go through. If you are a winter person, then learn to love the summer with all its heat and humidity and vice versa. Recognize that humans generally never miss or long for anything until they can't have it or until they lose access to it. You don't appreciate freedom until you lose it. You don't notice or miss your loved ones' presence in your life until you no longer have them. You don't appreciate your health until you become sick. You don't appreciate being able to walk until you no longer can walk, and so the list goes on. Therefore, for you to love and appreciate the summer heat and humidity, you will need to live in a constant, never-ending winter. Then and only then will you be able to realize that any activity or experience that you go through in life can teach you or bring about something new so long as you spend the proper time finishing and going through them. Hence, avoid being ungrateful for things you have and things you are and can do. Never go through life without enjoying every action and activity you do or are involved in.

Your life becomes filled with bad routines without requiring your approval. You unwillingly become chained and confined by some rules and guidelines while going through life with its different experiences and activities. You never stop to even think about those rules and guidelines and how they came to be a huge part of your life. You will go as far as thinking and believing that this is how life is supposed to go, and you will attribute those confining guidelines and rules to anything and everything but yourself. Yet, if you want to point the finger and blame someone for those chains and confining rules and guidelines, look no further than yourself. Those guidelines are coming from you and only you. It's saddening that you get only one life, and yet you are willingly chaining yourself with bogus rules and guidelines without even contemplating them, testing, or negotiating them. You are giving control of your life to the cycle of life and to other people and their ambiguous rules and guidelines they want to enforce on all humanity even though no two humans in this universe are identical, not even siblings or twins.

What differentiates a bad routine from a good one?

If it doesn't spark desire, and you need to drag yourself into it. When it's starting to affect your appetite for living, eating, and sleeping negatively. When you wake up every day feeling miserable just because of its existence in your life, then it's a bad routine. On the other hand, a good routine is the complete opposite, filled with desire, appetite for living and eating, and going out and about. It pushes you to wake up every day, the excitement and energy running through you. It gives you a positive push to experience new challenges and see the beauty in everything in life.

Additionally, there are a lot of entities, rules, and guidelines in life that contribute to your having a fast-paced world and joyless life. Entities such as work, kids, family, traditions, cultures, and health are all some aspects of your life that contribute to you having a fast-paced life filled with bad routines from the time you wake up to the time you sleep and so on to the next day. You need to get rid of any bad routines in your life and have a life filled with good routines. Slow down your world and try to enjoy more of it by changing your bad routines and turning them into more spontaneous activities. You do that by breaking some or all the rules which are chaining you and restricting you from having a joyous life.

Stop your world every now and then and smell the roses. There are many ways in which you can slow down your world and turn your bad routines into good ones, just by embracing and integrating them into your life. By embracing and injecting simple changes into your life, you introduce a small effect that can snowball into a significant change. Those changes you introduce will affect a variety of actions and activities, ranging from small, with low-effect actions and events to significant with huge-effect actions and events. For example, instead of waking up late, wake up early. Instead of buying your morning coffee, make it at home. Instead of driving to work, bike. Instead of rushing through traffic, use traffic and stoplights to watch your surroundings and meditate. Instead of recording a concert on your phone, put down your phone and enjoy the moment and dance through the show (unless, of course, you are a bad dancer, then please just nod and enjoy the concert without dancing). Don't just adhere to traditions, culture, rules, and guidelines just because you were brought up practicing and adhering to them. All traditions and cultures have rules and guidelines for everything that you are expected to follow to appease those people in your life, relatives or not, who usually push those rules and guidelines down your throat. A lot of these rules and guidelines are meant to restrict your life. They are there to control how much and what type of happiness and joy you can have in your life. So, decide to break your mental chains by rejecting those rules and guidelines. All that you need for you to inject joy and happiness into your life and to break those bad routines is not coming from the outside or from following rules and guidelines, but it's coming from within you.

Slowing down your world is a decision that you will have to make and work hard to achieve, and no one else will help you in doing so. It will require a great commitment and a greater attention to detail for you to be able to catch yourself when you relapse or revert to your bad routines and old habits. If it is your work that is forcing you to slip into a fast-paced world and bad routines, then you can start with merely just changing the method in which you go to work, by riding the bus or biking to work, or you can try driving to work using a new route. While at your work, if you are used to work sitting on a chair, start standing up to work. If the issue is your job itself, don't be afraid to look for a different job that satisfies your passion and desires, which allows you to see the beauty around you. Additionally, if it is your kids who are driving your fast-paced world and bad routines, then you can simply put them up for adoption, or if you really love them, you can include them on your journey to a slower world. For example, instead of putting them to bed after dinner, teach them to load the dishwasher or the laundry machine. If they are still babies, you can still include them by sleeping when they sleep and waking when they wake. This way, if they wake up in the middle of the night, you would still have gotten enough sleep, and you won't wake up the next day tired and fatigued. These changes to your life routines, whether at work or home with your family and kids, are not huge or life-changing by any stretch. However, when combining all of them and any other activity like them, they will accumulate into significant changes in your life and eventually will help you in slowing down and in injecting some joy and happiness into your life and world.

Tips and suggestions for slowing down your world and finding joy:

- Commit yourself to slow down your world to enjoy it while making sure to strive for your own balanced pace to allow yourself to enjoy it fully.

- Treat every new day as your last, making sure to cherish, appreciate, and celebrate every second of it, regardless of the type of activity you are doing, be it working, driving, eating, or even bird watching.

- Don't wait until that day comes when you realize that you have more past than you have future, for you to learn how to live your life in the moment and to have a greater appreciation for everything in your life, the smaller things before the big things.

- Teach yourself to live in the present and avoid thinking of things that happened or things that need to be done.

- Push back against normalizing your bad routines and habits. Avoid following all the societal and cultural rules and guidelines just because they exist but rather because you can see joy and happiness in them.

- Decide to regain control over your life by forcing new experiences and constant changes into it. Doing that, regardless of how big or small the changes are, will help you inject life into it more often.

Chapter SIXTEEN

Reaching success or failures, all for and because of love

"

Allow yourself to find love and allow love to find you.

Love can make or break you. Yet, if you want to do something significant with your life, you will need it. Love is a combination of feelings and emotions. Depending on the person you are giving love or showing love to, your love will have a different combination between some or all of these feelings and emotions, starting with communication, respect, understanding, desires, and acceptance. Keep in mind that love is not the same as desire, and even though you might confuse the two, desire at its core is different from love. Desire is when you go to the ocean to ride the waves, while love is when you go to the ocean to cherish the silence. With desires, you feed, nourish, and satisfy your mental and physical needs and wants, whereas, with love, you feed, nourish, and satisfy your heart and spiritual needs and wants, for all of your being.

You have always been taught that in life, one plus one is equal to two, and that might be true in almost everything except when it comes to love. One person loves another person, and they become a unit. So, make sure not to go through life without having experienced that type of love, the type that lets you feel what the other person is feeling without a word being spoken. When your loved ones are happy, you feel their happiness, and you are filled with joy. When they are sad, you feel their sorrow. Love is not butterflies and nervousness because butterflies and nervousness are only signs. These signs show up with attraction and before love. However, what comes after these signs is real love. After those butterflies and nervousness fade away, and you are still there, you will realize that what you have is real love, and then it's going to be up to your imagination to find ways to keep those butterflies and all that love running hot in your life.

Love can take you to great heights in happiness where no drugs or anything else can take you. Love can take you to heights in success; no other education or talent can take you to. It can be the driving force for your continued success and can act as the primary nourishment for your inspiration. This love can be a love for a spouse or a soulmate, but it is not limited to only those two. It can be your love for your parents, kids, self, country, or even your love for life. No matter the person or thing that you love, your love radiates from the same place. You show and give love to certain people or things, care about them, and you want them happy in your life, proud and safe not only because you know you love them but also because you love yourself. Regardless of whether your love is for people, animals, other things in your life, they all can be the main entity that stokes your fire and pushes you toward new heights. Naturally, anything in this life that takes you to new heights or makes you high has a side effect, and love is no different than any other drug when it comes to having side effects. Hence, love can also take you to lows and slumps no other obstacle nor pain can take you to, so tread carefully when opening yourself and your heart to love.

Love is like a train leaving the station, and you need to get on it. Otherwise, you will miss it. The train will not wait for you, and neither will love. So, make sure to keep your eyes and heart open, and be looking for love to catch that train of love. Finding love is easy, just look around, and you will find a person or a thing that you love. However, finding a love that takes you to different heights in life and success is hard. Yet, it's all in your hands and within your reach. You just need to be looking for it. Look around and observe people and things surrounding you to know who and what you love, to see and identify who loves you back, and know that the train of love will not wait for Your Highness to notice it. So, make sure never to lose the people or the things you love in life before taking time to appreciate how much love they have for you, or without telling, professing, and showing them how much love you have for them.

In life, you look for things to hate about people around you, about yourself, and the world around you. You hate the way someone is acting around you at work, or the way someone in your family talks and thinks. You hate the way they decide to live their lives. When you can't find someone or something else to hate in others, you turn to hating things about yourself. If you are short in height, you hate that, and if you are tall, you hate being tall. If your frame is small, you hate that your bones are showing, and if your frame is big, you hate that not enough bones are showing. You hate everything about the way you look or the way you dress. There are so many reasons that corner you into thinking negatively and pushes you into looking for things to hate on. It can be your lack of confidence and self-worth, your lack of direction or life goals and purpose. No matter the reason for your hate, trying to find things to hate about others, yourself, and life will only lead you to a miserable life, lacking happiness and joy and full of gloomy days.

Thus, to avoid going deeper into that cycle of hate and gloominess, you should reverse that curse by teaching yourself how to find the good things about the people around you, about yourself, and life in general. One thing always to remember is that your hate toward the way others think, talk, or decide to live their lives will not do or change anything about the way they talk or live. Rather, it's going only to affect you and not in a good way. The more hate you have for others, yourself, and for life, the less room you will have for love, happiness, and joy. Loving a person, be it a friend, a family member, a spouse, or a partner requires you to accept their imperfections. Understand that no one in this world is without deficiencies or imperfections, not you, and not anyone else. Therefore, never have any expectation of perfection when giving or showing your love to anyone. Choose to let others live their lives the way they see fit for themselves, and if you must be with or around them, then learn and decide to love the good things about them and within them.

Furthermore, when it comes to loving yourself, just know that you can always work on improving yourself physically, spiritually, and mentally to get to a better place from where you are currently. However, while doing that, you should find things you love and enjoy right where you are now because love is like a muscle that needs to be trained, worked on, and exercised to keep on improving and growing. If you can't find a lot to love where you are right now, you can at least try loving the process of working on improving yourself physically, emotionally, and mentally, because doing that will keep your love muscle agile and ready for expansion. Furthermore, recognize that you always get from your world what you put into it. Therefore, the more love you have and show for yourself, for others, and for life, the more that love muscle grows, and the more love you will receive back from the world around you.

Additionally, you, alongside everyone else in this life, can find love, and you can also allow love to find you. To do so, you just need to decide that you want love to exist within you and in your life. In your journey to finding love, first and foremost, you start with loving yourself since you cannot love someone or something without having a love for yourself. You cannot give that which you don't have. If you don't have love for yourself, then you won't be able to give or show love to others. Therefore, before trying to find someone to love or that loves you, sit and observe yourself to find something that you love about yourself, be it your personality, appearance, or even the way your brain works or thinks. Once you find that which you love about yourself and once you decide to appreciate it and admire it, it will be like a beaming light shining through you with confidence, and you will not be able to hide it. Eventually, others will be able to feel it, see it, and relate to it, and then be able to love it and love you for it.

With love in your life, you can become happy, strong, and motivated, but you can also become sad, weak, and heartbroken. How love affects you and your life all depends on how much control you have over your love logic or love's agent. You love a spouse, and they cheat on you physically or emotionally and break your heart. By doing so, they can break you and make you feel low and sad, but instead of allowing that love to make you feel sad and take you to lows you are not used to or can't even handle, you can decide to use their cheating and reverse its lows and sadness to heights and happiness. You lose your beloved parents or one of them, but instead of allowing that loss to take you to lows and sadness, you look and search for your parents' love from within the tragedy surrounding you and use it to take you to heights and happiness. Reversing and controlling the effect of heartbreak, grief, and anguish will require great control from you over your love agent. Becoming skilled at controlling your love agent will thrust you into a changed life, full of joy and unlimited happiness and love. Once you embrace and love everything that is you, the good and the not so good, and once you start looking for things to love in others and in life, your life will take a sharp turn for the better, and you will be able to wave goodbye to your gloomy days.

Some methods and techniques to find love that will take you to different heights in life and success:

- Take a few minutes from your super precious time and find three things you love about yourself, be it your personality, appearance, or way of thinking. Then in your daily routine, while standing in front of a mirror, washing your face or brushing teeth, repeat what you love about yourself.

- Once you find things to love about yourself, then and only then will others start noticing and loving those same things. By loving those things about yourself and showing confidence in yourself, you, in turn, make sure to highlight those things you love about yourself. Doing that will make it harder for others to miss or disregard them, and consequently harder for them not to fall in love with it and love you for it.

- Open yourself and your heart to experience love, for you to love, and to be loved.

- Profess, show, and speak your love to those whom you love. Not only should you allow them to know that you love them, but you should also empower them to profess their love for you.

- Accept people around you for who and what they are; stop setting expectations for them. Instead of highlighting things you hate about them, learn to find things you love about them and about life.

- Use your love for yourself, for others, and for life itself to get rid of your gloomy days. Exercise your control over your love agent and utilize it to bring in more happiness and joy into your life.

CHAPTER SEVENTEEN

Uncovering the bright side hiding within depression

"

No one in this world has it all, and neither do they have it all under control.

Understand that it's okay for you to be flawed and make mistakes. It's not at all bad if you ever feel depressed or overwhelmed by life and all the people and events within it. You are not the only one with these types of feelings and emotions, and it's not a sign of weakness or a sign of deficiency or failure. Having those feelings and emotions of depression and being overwhelmed shows that you care about yourself and who you became as a person and where you are in life. Caring this much in itself can be a sign of a colorful, bright future full of achievement and success. It's okay and sometimes even necessary for you to have blue days and to experience some form of depression. It's necessary because at the end of each depressing experience is one of two states of mind, either total insanity and unprecedented demise or self-realization and pure joy. So, you can succumb and accept being a causality of the negative force known as depression, or you can fight that negative force and try pushing yourself through it and come out with your sanity intact. Doing that will allow you to have a better understanding of that which lifts your spirit and injects light into your gloomy and blue days.

To rid yourself of that undesirable state and mood, you must turn to your faith, prayer, and meditation if you have those principles in your life, or you can and should always speak those feelings and emotions out by talking with a trusted friend or a specialist. Additionally, you must give yourself time to decompress and to meditate by either bringing yourself into a familiar comfort zone or by pushing yourself to the other end of the spectrum, outside your comfort zone. Doing either one of those techniques and choosing the extreme side of each will either take you into a familiar comfort zone that calms your mind and soul. Or it will inject some needed unfamiliarity and some exciting newness into your sphere of living and your life. You can choose to inject some nostalgic or spontaneous activities into your life. Nostalgic activities means doing something that will take you back to a familiar comfort zone, reminding you of a better time, such as listening to old or new music that takes your mind out of its current state into a better time. You can also try watching one of your favorite childhood cartoons or TV shows, which can also bring your mind to a more stable and a better time. Additionally, you can also try injecting into your life some spontaneous activities by pushing yourself outside your comfort zone with new experiences that have unknown and unpredictable results. Or you can have an ongoing, open-ended project doing an activity that you enjoy, be it writing, painting, or even video gaming, that you can fall back on when your mind is asking for that needed break. The goal behind that open-ended project is not achieving a milestone or reaching a result, but rather it's to give your mind much-needed downtime. Last but not least, you can try helping and aiding others with their issues, problems, and depression. Doing that and seeing others' issues and different types of struggle with depression can give you a bird's-eye view of your struggles and consequently help you in minimizing or moving past it.

The main goal of doing any of these techniques is to take yourself and your mind out of the negative space you're floating in, even if it's only for a short period. Each minute and any hour that your mind is not floating in that negative space is precious in your journey toward controlling your depression, minimizing it, and even defeating it. Using any one of these techniques will give you a better chance at injecting that needed minute or hour of decompression and temporary relief. Also, it will more than likely give your mind the space it needs to re-energize and recharge, allowing you to find peace with yourself and with any difficulty and issue in your life.

The worst thing that can happen to you is to die while you are still living, to be so depressed that you lose your appetite for speaking, laughing, and interacting. At that point, it's all about you, and no one else can take you out of that depressed state. It's about understanding your values, goals, and life purpose, or it's about finding them if you don't have any. Don't be quick to judge life as not worth living. Give yourself the time and the space to figure things out. Finding solace in that depression is a strong but ugly sign that you care about yourself, who you became, and where you are in life. Remember that your issues and problems are bigger in your own eyes than it is for others because you are the one feeling the weight and the madness of those issues and problems.

Tips and things to know when dealing with depression:

- Being depressed or overwhelmed by life and all the people and events within it is not a sign of weakness or deficiency or failure. You can be successful, rich, and famous and still suffer from depression.

- One positive thing that depression emphasizes is that you care about yourself and where you at in life.

- The main solution for depression lies within yourself. Understanding or finding your purpose in life and reaching a point of contentment with who you are mentally, physically, and emotionally will be your immunization against depression.

- Use your faith, prayers, and meditation if you have those principles in your life and make sure to speak those feelings and emotions out to a trusted friend or a specialist.

- Give yourself time to decompress and meditate by either bringing yourself into a familiar comfort zone or by pushing yourself outside your comfort zone.

- Try helping others with their issues with depression, because seeing others' struggle with depression can give you a bird's-eye view of your own struggles and consequently help you minimize or move past it.

CHAPTER EIGHTEEN

Living Beyond your death

"

You stop fearing death when you confront it.

Life is not just a breath you take or an action you make. Life is a never-ending story full of surprises and plot twists, and you are the hero and the villain of that story. Life is an open ocean full of heavy rains and waves and deadly storms. You can be the captain of your ship and sail through the open oceans and move from one port to another. You can paint your own life the way you see fit. As captain of your ship, you should aspire to live way beyond your death by leaving a legacy behind that will allow your memories to stand the test of time. You do that by writing your own life story optimizing all the power and capacities you own to go through life's different stages. You do that by humbling yourself through acquiring knowledge in all its forms and by inspiring others to aspire to do what's good for humanity. Moreover, you do that by standing up for, protecting, and caring about others' wellbeing and dignity as much if not more than your own. Doing all that will give your story the power it needs to ingratiate itself into people's present and future. It will create the resiliency it needs to stand the test of time.

A mistake that keeps you from living an exemplary life and leaving a good legacy behind is when you wait for the unknown and lose sight of the known. You overlook what you know and what's within your view, you never appreciate it, nor do you celebrate it. All because you are waiting for something else to happen or for you to get something else for yourself. Your eventual death is not the problem; rather, it's your present nonliving and lifeless existence. Guarantee yourself a vibrant existence full of life and joy by aspiring and working toward leaving an inspiring legacy. Learn to enjoy the process of everything or every experience you have or do. For you to live beyond your death and leave a good legacy behind, you will have to go through life's different stages, searching and researching until you find your truth. For without knowing and understanding your truth, your legacy will not find a solid ground to stand on. You go through life with its ups and downs and experience so many different stages. Stages such as the mental stage, the emotional stage, the spiritual stage, and the physical stage. These stages are an integral part of what makes you mature in your life and what allows you to live your life to the fullest. Each one of these stages will take you through different paths, directions, and experiences. Only by going through each one of them can you fully understand the meaning and purpose of your life. Understanding and grasping the meaning of your life will help you find your truth and unlock the beauty in your life.

There is the mental stage that you endure and navigate through in life by reading, learning, writing, acting, and reacting then reflecting. You read and gain knowledge, and then you learn how to live your life utilizing that knowledge. Then you write to build upon your understanding, and you act and react to all the different challenges and experiences life takes you through. Finally, you sit down, reflect, and then go at it again by reading, writing, acting, and reacting, then reflecting and repeating the cycle so you can grow and strengthen yourself mentally. Lacking one of the items listed above will only delay your mental evolution. However, without the act of reflecting, the chance of your mental maturation is slim to none. Setting aside time to reflect on yourself and your life is vital for your mental maturation. It allows you to see, understand, and realize your lesson learned from all the experiences you went through and from all the good and bad choices you made.

Additionally, there is also the emotional stage by experiencing happiness and joy, sadness and heartaches that life throws at you and using those experiences to enhance and mold your emotional intelligence. You mature emotionally by deciding to fill your life with joy and laughter by doing and seeking good, but most importantly, by sharing your joy and happiness with others. Furthermore, there is the spiritual stage by praying, meditating, and observing the world and nature around you. You mature spiritually by finding and filling your life with all the beauty you can within this life and this world. You mature spiritually by appreciating your existence and by finding and working on your purpose in life and being true to it. Last but not least, one final stage to complete the stages of your life is the physical stage. Your body needs to go through some physical activities and experiences like walking, running, the same way your mind and soul need their nourishment.

As you go through these life stages, you will learn how to utilize and benefit from each stage that you go through. However, going through all those stages alone will not leave a legacy that inspires others. In addition, you will also need a healthy amount of decency, dignity, and sacrifice in your life for your quest to leaving a good legacy behind to materialize. You, as a living being, are born with dignity. You don't have to look for it or learn to pick it up. You must learn how to protect it and never lose it. On the other hand, that is not the case when it comes to decency and being humble. As a human being, you are born thinking that the earth does not rotate around its axis or the sun, but rather it's rotating around you. If you ever needed proof of that, just go ahead and ask your parents about how humble or decent you were when you were a baby, a kid, or even a teenager, and you will learn how wicked and self-centered you were in all the different stages of your upbringing. By going through life's different stages, you will pick up the proper knowledge and experiences and learn how to humble yourself and be decent while maintaining your dignity. Yet, one thing will stand between you and humbling yourself and being decent: your decision. You hold the power to decide whether your knowledge and life experiences, with all the gains and losses, should humble you and make you a decent person while still maintaining your self-worth and dignity, or not.

Additionally, sacrificing for the betterment and the advancement of your community, the people in it, and the world around you, is another way you can live beyond your death. Sacrifices can include but are not limited to time, money and resources, freedom, or even your life. Any sacrifice for the betterment of the community and world around you will ingratiate your name into the present, future, and past of that community and world. One thing to keep in mind while traveling along the road of leaving a legacy behind; all the things adored by the eyes will eventually cease to be admired. However, anything that has both a story and a history that can reach the heart and which the soul can feel will be forever be admired, and their effect will never be measured nor quantified. The word "sacrifice" has a negative connotation because of its association with receiving less or not as much of an object, or an entity. However, the truth is that the more you sacrifice, the more you will be satisfied and fulfilled. In life, you are willing to sacrifice if you care deeply about something, a person, a goal, a dream, or an idea. Therefore, when you sacrifice for that person's wellbeing and happiness or when you sacrifice for the materialization of that dream or vision, you are ultimately working toward bringing satisfaction to yourself.

Sacrifices can differ from person to another or from one situation to another. You can sacrifice your time teaching and enlightening others, or you can also create some art to inspire and lift others' spirit and imagination. You can sacrifice your money and resources to develop a solution for a problem or a vaccine for a disease. Furthermore, you can sacrifice your freedom by standing up against all forms of inequality and physical or mental slavery. Lastly, you can sacrifice your life standing up and fighting for the rights and dignity of others within your community and the whole world. Throughout history, there are many examples of individuals who sacrificed so many different things in their lives to lift the community they live in or the field they worked in. Therefore, some people and their many sacrifices have been infused into people memories and their history, present, and future. Their work and sacrifices are being relished to this day, and some even being taught in schools. Their names are celebrated as heroes, each in their own field, but they all are heroes in the field of humanity, for all the good and the sacrifices they offered for the betterment of their communities and the world around them.

You will go through these stages and not necessarily in the order they are listed in. Therefore, live your life to the fullest and remember to observe the people in your life, because some people show up in your life as a blessing while others as a lesson. So, make sure to be grateful for the blessings while learning from all the lessons. Aspire and commit yourself to leave a good legacy behind by humbling yourself and being decent while maintaining your dignity and caring about others' wellbeing and dignities. Only then will you be able to engrave your name into people's memories and their future.

Finally, to keep yourself grounded and in check, learn to strip every material thing you have or own, be it money, a car, or a house, and then save an imaginative picture of what's left somewhere in that big head of yours and keep it within your sight at all time. When you strip all the material things you own or have, you are then left with all the important items and entities that define you: your hard work, your good deeds, and your thinking mind. Every once in a while, pull that imaginative picture from where it is stored and use it as a measuring stick. A measuring stick between your current situation and who you are, versus where and who you want to be. If you feel that you are not content with where you are, nor are you happy with who you became as a person, then use that picture and that discontentment as motivation to push yourself to do more with yourself and with your time. Doing that will make it a habit for you to be a better person toward yourself and other living beings, and it will make it possible for your legacy to be cemented.

Some tips and guidelines toward becoming a better you and creating an inspiring legacy:

- Every life on this earth has a purpose and an equal effect on others' lives. So, learn to appreciate and care about others' lives, wellbeing, and dignities as much as you care about your own life and dignity.

- In life, there is no loss except losing yourself. Losing every material thing you have and own to save yourself is not a loss, rather it's the only big win you need.

- The best lesson that you can learn will always come from personal loss and personal breakdowns or illness. So, learn to take those losses and failures with acceptance and resiliency, instead of allowing them to stop you from reaching your goals and dreams. Use them as fuel for moving forward.

- For you to live beyond your death, you will need to make sure to guard and protect others' dignities as much as you guard and protect your own. Living your life with your dignity intact, humbling yourself, and sacrificing when and what you can, are the required tokens on your road toward leaving an inspiring legacy behind.

CHAPTER NINETEEN

Succeeding in life

> **"**
>
> Try always to be the person who plants the seed instead of being the one looking to harvest it. Plant the seed of ethics, good morals, culture, and decency.

Be patient and plan accordingly

Learn to guard yourself physically, mentally, and emotionally by exercising patience in all that you do and in any challenge that you face in life. Certainly, being patient with all that you do or face does not mean avoiding being spontaneous, nor it means staying away from taking any risk in your life. On the contrary, it means taking all the required, calculated risks for you to grow, for your business to expand its reach, or for anything else that you are involved in to flourish and develop. Taking those risks with the proper control, planning, and studying will give you the required confidence to push you through any challenges you face and will put you on the path toward reaching and gaining the desired results from taking those risks. Additionally, understanding your limits and breaking points, be it physical, emotional, mental, and even financial, will guard you from all the negativity that surrounds each risk you take. It will prepare you with a shield that will minimize the effect or hurt coming from those risks.

"Follow what you are good at and become great at it. If it happens to be the same as your passion, then you have hit the jackpot."

Confidence is the only beauty product you will ever need

Having unshakable confidence in yourself and what you do is one of the most rewarding characteristics you can have. Having self-confidence can accelerate your path to success in everything you do. However, being able to control your confidence will give you the power not only to humble yourself but will allow you to have an everlasting success and a legendary legacy. Reaching that point where you are not only able to project confidence in all that you do but also control it is not an easy feat. You will have to work on understanding yourself, loving it, or at least being content with it in all its aspects, be it physical, mental, or emotional. Moreover, you will need to maintain your eagerness to learn about yourself and about life. The power of knowledge, alongside your willingness to help and mentor others, will not only benefit them, but it will also benefit you by boosting your confidence and allowing you to mature in life. Aspire to reach a point where you can accept that each belief and all knowledge that you have can, at some point, be flawed or wrong. This way, you will always be willing to modify your stance on certain subjects in life, and you will be open to new lessons that life will throw at you along the way.

Balance your life to control it properly

More often than not, you will get lost in your world and all the issues within it. You will forget all the good things, physical or not, that you have, and all the good things happening to you or that has happened to you in the past. Recognize that real life is not about receiving all the time, but rather it's a mix between giving and receiving. Therefore, you should learn to balance those acts of giving and receiving in your life for you to be able to take control of it. Furthermore, understand that having control over your life or part of it does not necessarily equate to properly understanding it and knowing how it works or how it supposed to function. For example, you can buy a car with a manual gearbox, and you can be good at driving it using the steering wheel. Yet, if you cannot drive a manual gear, then your ability to control that car is useless. Therefore, when deciding to take control of every small or big thing in your life, make sure that you know how to steer and navigate your life through all the challenges and experiences, you go through. Focus your energy toward reaching your destinations and achieving all your goals. Stop looking for excuses for not moving forward with your life, because life is not going to wait for you, nor is it going to wait for your situation to get better. You will need to understand that life is not a problem to be solved but it's meant to be lived and experienced with all its ups and downs.